MUST-HAVE Grammar

BOOK 3

HANILEDU.PUBLISHER

이 책의 특징

1 45개 필수 핵심 문법
- 9개의 공부법을 적용한 필수 핵심 문법으로 전권을 구성하였습니다.
- 문법, 글쓰기, 성적향상 그리고 영어 활용성을 동시에 해결할 수 있는 문법 순서와 내용으로 구성하였습니다.

2 KEY POINT 문법 설명
- 간결한 구성과 이해하기 쉬운 명쾌한 설명으로 구성하였습니다.
- 선생님과 학생들 모두 요점 이해와 파악이 쉽도록 꼭 필요한 POINT 설명만 담았습니다.

3 단계별 다양한 연습문제
- 배운 문법을 정확히 익히고 최대한 활용할 수 있도록 충분한 양의 연습문제를 제공하였습니다.
- 9개의 공부법 적용 : 단계별로 제시되는 다양한 연습문제를 통해 수업 집중도가 올라가고 문법 습득이 빨라집니다.

4 문법에서 쓰기까지 체계적 구성
- Grammar Point(문법 학습) → Grammar Exercise(연습문제) → Writing Practice(문장 및 문단쓰기) → Review(긴 문단쓰기)로 단계별 문법 연습과 쓰기 연습을 할 수 있습니다.

5 서술형, 논술형 평가 대비
- 다양한 쓰기, 단어, 읽기, 문법 문제를 통해 서술형과 논술형 수업과 시험을 체계적으로 대비할 수 있습니다.

6 장르별 영어 글쓰기
- 여러 가지 장르의 글을 통해 현장감 있는 영어를 배울 수 있도록 하였고, 사고력 확장에 도움을 줍니다.
- 편지글(Letter), 게시글(Notice), 리포트(Report), 에세이(Essay), 묘사하는 글쓰기(Descriptive essay), 연극 대본(Play script), 서사적 글쓰기(Narrative essay) 등과 같은 다양한 장르의 글이 포함되어 있습니다.

MUST-HAVE Grammar

구성과 특징

Part 1 Grammar Point

- 표 또는 수식을 활용하여, 문법 사항을 한 눈에 보기 쉽게 정리
- 명확한 핵심 문법 설명과 실용적인 예문

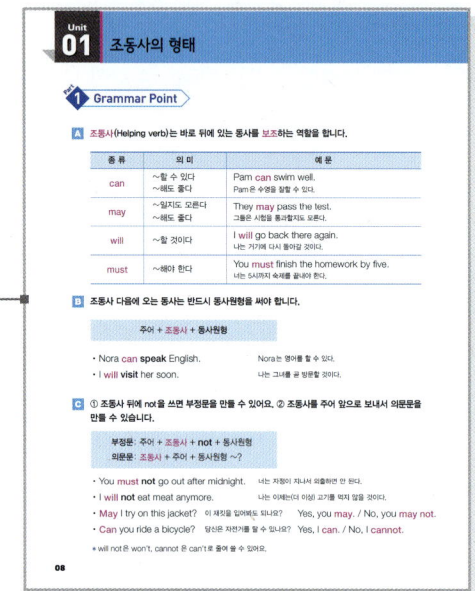

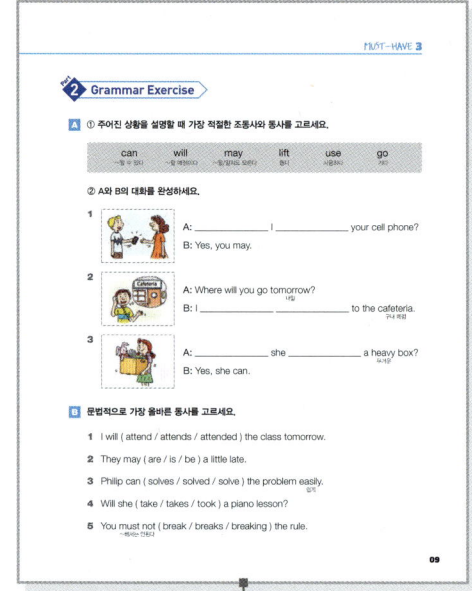

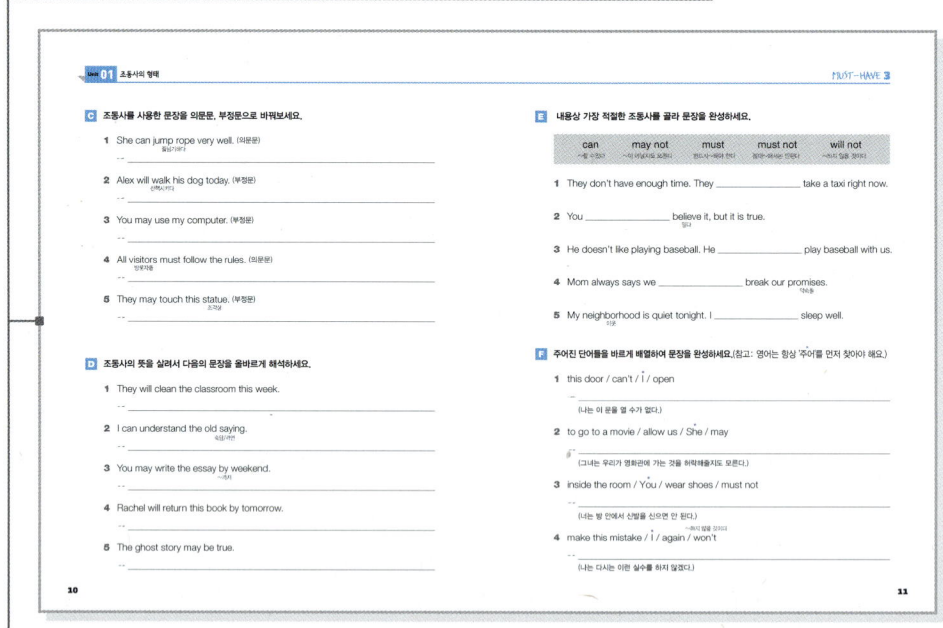

Part 2 Grammar Exercise

- 다양한 문법 연습문제를 단계별로 제시
- 핵심 문법의 체계적 연습

Part 3
Writing Practice

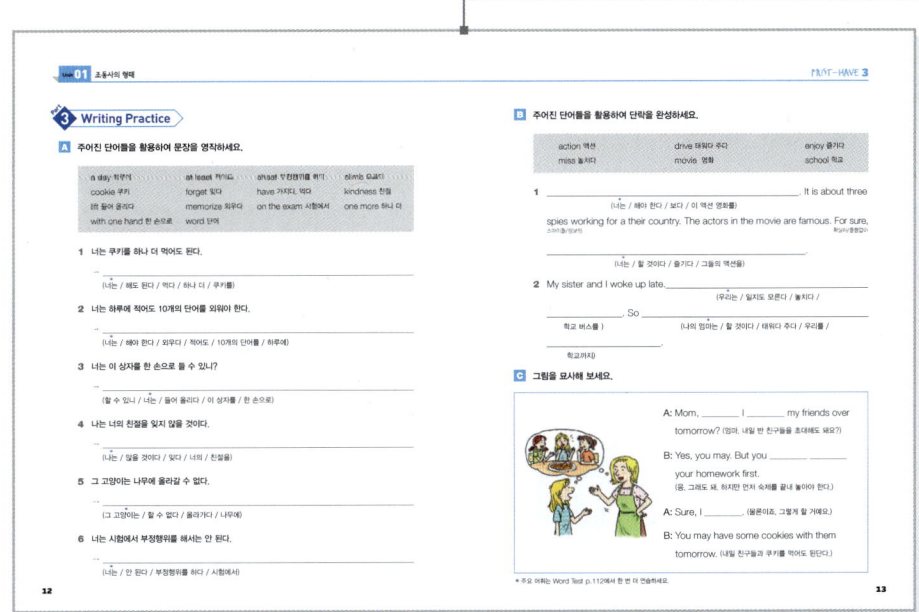

- 핵심 문법을 활용한 문장 및 짧은 단락 쓰기를 통해 글쓰기의 기초를 마련
- 다양한 쓰기 문제를 통해 서술형 평가 유형에 대비

Review

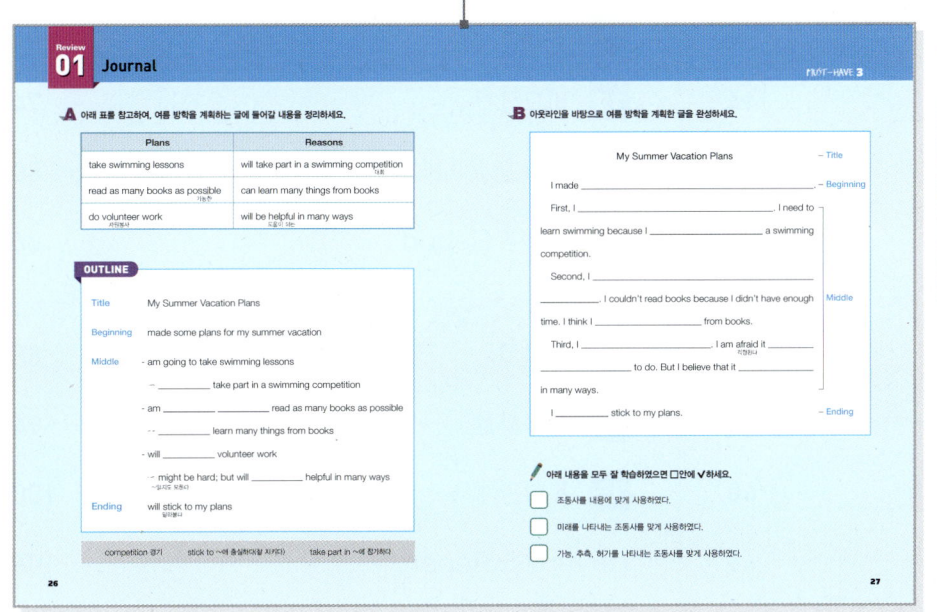

- 핵심 문법을 적용한 완성된 글쓰기 연습
- 다양한 장르별 글쓰기 연습
- 글쓰기 후 핵심 문법 재확인

Appendix	불규칙 변화 동사표, 부사접속사 종류
Word Test	Writing Practice에서 학습한 단어들을 점검해 볼 수 있는 단어 테스트
Answer Key	Unit별 연습문제와 Review의 정답

Contents MUST-HAVE Grammar

Book 3

1 조동사의 형태	8
2 미래의 조동사	14
3 가능·추측·허가의 조동사	20
Review 1 Journal	26
4 의무의 조동사	28
5 습관의 조동사	34
6 부사절을 만드는 접속사 1	40
Review 2 Journal	46
7 부사절을 만드는 접속사 2	48
8 수여동사	54
9 지각동사와 사역동사	60
Review 3 Narrative Essay	66

10 현재완료	68
11 비교급	74
12 수와 양을 나타내기	80
Review 4 Report	86
13 명사절	88
14 형용사절	94
15 복합관계사	100
Review 5 Report	106
Appendix	108
Word Test	111
Answer Key	121

Book 1

1. 형용사 + 명사
2. 주어 + be동사 + 형용사
3. 명사의 단수와 중복, 관사

Review 1

4. 주어 + be동사 + 명사
5. 주어 + 일반동사 + 명사
6. 주어 + 동사 + 형용사 + 명사

Review 2

7. 전치사
8. 전치사구
9. 다수의 전치사구

Review 3

10. There is / There are
11. 부사; 형용사의 변형
12. 빈도부사

Review 4

13. 동명사
14. 현재분사
15. 현재진행형

Review 5

Appendix

Word Test

Answer Key

Book 2

1. 의문문의 do
2. 부정문의 do not
3. 강조의 do

Review 1

4. 인칭대명사
5. 의문사가 있는 의문문
6. in order to / to

Review 2

7. too ~ to / enough to
8. to부정사를 형용사처럼 쓰기
9. to부정사를 부사처럼 쓰기

Review 3

10. to부정사·동명사를 목적어로 쓰기
11. to부정사를 목적격 보어로 쓰기
12. -thing + 형용사

Review 4

13. 과거분사 만들기
14. 수동태
15. 부정대명사

Review 5

Appendix

Word Test

Answer Key

Unit 01 조동사의 형태

Part 1 Grammar Point

A 조동사(Helping verb)는 바로 뒤에 있는 동사를 보조하는 역할을 합니다.

종류	의미	예문
can	~할 수 있다 ~해도 좋다	Pam **can** swim well. Pam은 수영을 잘할 수 있다.
may	~일지도 모른다 ~해도 좋다	They **may** pass the test. 그들은 시험을 통과할지도 모른다.
will	~할 것이다	I **will** go back there again. 나는 거기에 다시 돌아갈 것이다.
must	~해야 한다	You **must** finish the homework by five. 너는 5시까지 숙제를 끝내야 한다.

B 조동사 다음에 오는 동사는 반드시 동사원형을 써야 합니다.

> 주어 + 조동사 + 동사원형

- Nora **can speak** English.　　　　Nora는 영어를 할 수 있다.
- I **will visit** her soon.　　　　나는 그녀를 곧 방문할 것이다.

C ① 조동사 뒤에 not을 쓰면 부정문을 만들 수 있어요. ② 조동사를 주어 앞으로 보내서 의문문을 만들 수 있습니다.

> 부정문: 주어 + 조동사 + **not** + 동사원형
> 의문문: 조동사 + 주어 + 동사원형 ~?

- You **must not** go out after midnight.　너는 자정이 지나서 외출하면 안 된다.
- I **will not** eat meat anymore.　나는 이제는(더 이상) 고기를 먹지 않을 것이다.
- **May** I try on this jacket?　이 재킷을 입어봐도 되나요?　Yes, you **may**. / No, you **may not**.
- **Can** you ride a bicycle?　당신은 자전거를 탈 수 있나요?　Yes, I **can**. / No, I **cannot**.

* will not은 won't, cannot은 can't로 줄여 쓸 수 있어요.

Part 2 Grammar Exercise

A ① 주어진 상황을 설명할 때 가장 적절한 조동사와 동사를 고르세요.

can	will	may	lift	use	go
~할 수 있다	~할 예정이다	~할/일지도 모른다	들다	사용하다	가다

② A와 B의 대화를 완성하세요.

1.
A: _____ I _____ your cell phone?
B: Yes, you may.

2.
A: Where will you go tomorrow? (내일)
B: I _____ _____ to the cafeteria. (구내 매점)

3. A: _____ she _____ a heavy box? (무거운)
B: Yes, she can.

B 문법적으로 가장 올바른 동사를 고르세요.

1. I will (attend / attends / attended) the class tomorrow.

2. They may (are / is / be) a little late.

3. Philip can (solves / solved / solve) the problem easily. (쉽게)

4. Will she (take / takes / took) a piano lesson?

5. You must not (break / breaks / breaking) the rule.
(~해서는 안된다)

Unit 01 조동사의 형태

C 조동사를 사용한 문장을 의문문, 부정문으로 바꿔보세요.

1. She can jump rope very well. (의문문)
   줄넘기하다
   → _____

2. Alex will walk his dog today. (부정문)
   산책시키다
   → _____

3. You may use my computer. (부정문)
   → _____

4. All visitors must follow the rules. (의문문)
   방문자들
   → _____

5. They may touch this statue. (부정문)
   조각상
   → _____

D 조동사의 뜻을 살려서 다음의 문장을 올바르게 해석하세요.

1. They will clean the classroom this week.
   → _____

2. I can understand the old saying.
   속담/격언
   → _____

3. You may write the essay by weekend.
   ~까지
   → _____

4. Rachel will return this book by tomorrow.
   → _____

5. The ghost story may be true.
   → _____

MUST-HAVE 3

E 내용상 가장 적절한 조동사를 골라 문장을 완성하세요.

can	may not	must	must not	will not
~할 수 있다	~이 아닐지도 모른다	반드시~해야 한다	절대~해서는 안된다	~하지 않을 것이다

1 They don't have enough time. They _____ take a taxi right now.

2 You _____ believe it, but it is true.
   　　　　　　　　믿다

3 He doesn't like playing baseball. He _____ play baseball with us.

4 Mom always says we _____ break our promises.
   　　　　　　　　　　　　　　　　　　　　　　약속들

5 My neighborhood is quiet tonight. I _____ sleep well.
   　　이웃

F 주어진 단어들을 바르게 배열하여 문장을 완성하세요. (참고: 영어는 항상 '주어'를 먼저 찾아야 해요.)

1 this door / can't / I / open

   → _____

   (나는 이 문을 열 수가 없다.)

2 to go to a movie / allow us / She / may

   → _____

   (그녀는 우리가 영화관에 가는 것을 허락해줄지도 모른다.)

3 inside the room / You / wear shoes / must not

   → _____

   (너는 방 안에서 신발을 신으면 안 된다.)

4 make this mistake / I / again / won't
   　　　　　　　　　　　　　　　　~하지 않을 것이다

   → _____

   (나는 다시는 이런 실수를 하지 않겠다.)

Unit 01 조동사의 형태

Part 3 Writing Practice

A 주어진 단어들을 활용하여 문장을 영작하세요.

a day 하루에	at least 적어도	cheat 부정행위를 하다	climb 오르다
cookie 쿠키	forget 잊다	have 가지다, 먹다	kindness 친절
lift 들어 올리다	memorize 외우다	on the exam 시험에서	one more 하나 더
with one hand 한 손으로	word 단어		

1 너는 쿠키를 하나 더 먹어도 된다.

→ _____

(너는 / 해도 된다* / 먹다 / 하나 더 / 쿠키를)

2 너는 하루에 적어도 10개의 단어를 외워야 한다.

→ _____

(너는 / 해야 한다* / 외우다 / 적어도 / 10개의 단어를 / 하루에)

3 너는 이 상자를 한 손으로 들 수 있니?

→ _____

(할 수 있니 / 너는 / 들어 올리다* / 이 상자를 / 한 손으로)

4 나는 너의 친절을 잊지 않을 것이다.

→ _____

(나는 / 않을 것이다* / 잊다 / 너의 / 친절을)

5 그 고양이는 나무에 올라갈 수 없다.

→ _____

(그 고양이는 / 할 수 없다* / 올라가다 / 나무에)

6 너는 시험에서 부정행위를 해서는 안 된다.

→ _____

(너는 / 안 된다* / 부정행위를 하다 / 시험에서)

MUST-HAVE 3

B 주어진 단어들을 활용하여 단락을 완성하세요.

| action 액션 | drive 태워다 주다 | enjoy 즐기다 |
| miss 놓치다 | movie 영화 | school 학교 |

1 _____. It is about three
   (너는 / 해야 한다 / 보다 / 이 액션 영화를)

spies working for a their country. The actors in the movie are famous. For sure,
스파이들/정보원   확실히/틀림없이

_____.
   (너는 / 할 것이다 / 즐기다 / 그들의 액션을)

2 My sister and I woke up late. _____
                                (우리는 / 일지도 모른다 / 놓치다 /

_____. So _____
학교 버스를)   (나의 엄마는 / 할 것이다 / 태워다 주다 / 우리를 /

_____.
학교까지)

C 그림을 묘사해 보세요.

A: Mom, _____ I _____ my friends over tomorrow? (엄마, 내일 반 친구들을 초대해도 돼요?)

B: Yes, you may. But you _____ _____ your homework first.
(응, 그래도 돼. 하지만 먼저 숙제를 끝내 놓아야 한다.)

A: Sure, I _____. (물론이죠, 그렇게 할 거예요.)

B: You may have some cookies with them tomorrow. (내일 친구들과 쿠키를 먹어도 된단다.)

＊ 주요 어휘는 Word Test p.112에서 한 번 더 연습하세요.

Unit 02 미래의 조동사

Part 1 Grammar Point

A 조동사 will은 미래에 할 일을 말합니다. 주로 '~할(일) 것이다'의 의미를 가집니다.

- I **will** leave tomorrow morning. — 나는 내일 아침 떠날 것이다.
- He **will** succeed because he works hard. — 그는 열심히 일하기 때문에 성공할 것이다.

*I will은 I'll로 I will not은 I won't로 줄여 쓸 수 있어요.

B be going to는 will처럼 미래를 나타내지만, will보다 일어날 확률이 더 높은 미래를 말해요.

조동사	쓰 임	예 문
will	즉흥적인 계획이나 의지	• (The phone is ringing.) I **will** get it! (전화가 울림) 내가 (전화) 받을게요! • I am very tired now. I **will** take a short nap. 나는 지금 매우 피곤해. 잠깐 낮잠을 잘 거야.
be going to	미리 정해진 계획	• We **are going to** eat the pancakes. 우리는 팬케이크를 먹을 것이다. • He **is going to** visit his grandmother this vacation. 그는 이번 방학에 할머니를 뵈러 갈 것이다.

C will 뒤에 not, be동사 뒤에 not을 쓰면 부정문이 만들어 집니다.
의문문을 만들 때는 will과 be동사를 문장 맨 앞으로 보내면 됩니다.

조동사	부정문	의문문
will	주어 + will not (won't) + 동사원형	Will + 주어 + 동사원형~?
be going to	주어 + be동사 + not + going to + 동사원형	be동사 + 주어 + going to + 동사원형~?

부정
They **will not (won't)** see the tennis match. — 그들은 테니스 시합을 보지 않을 것이다.
She **is not going to** attend class today. — 그녀는 오늘 수업에 출석하지 않을 것이다.

의문
Will they see the tennis match? — 그들이 테니스 시합을 볼까요?
Is she **going to** attend class today? — 그녀는 오늘 수업에 출석할 건가요?

Part 2 Grammar Exercise

A ① 주어진 상황과 가장 잘 어울리는 조동사와 동사를 고르세요.

will	move	won't	going to
~할 예정이다	움직이다	~하지 않을 예정이다	~할 예정중(계획)

② A와 B의 대화를 완성하세요.

1 A: Can I have one more candy?
   B: No, you can't have any more. I _____ change my mind.
   마음/생각

2
   A: I am _____ go on a picnic this weekend.
   소풍을 가다
   B: I envy you.
   부러워하다

3
   A: _____ you help me _____ this sofa?
   B: Sure, I will help you.

B 동사의 쓰임이 올바른 것을 고르세요.

1 When are you (go / going) to study English?

2 He says, "I will (am / be) back soon."

3 She is not going to (skip / skipping) her classes.

4 I am going to (buy / bought) a car next month.

5 Tony is going (stay / to stay) at his grandma's tonight.

Unit 02 미래의 조동사

C be going to를 사용하여 미래에 더 확실하게 일어날 내용으로 바꾸세요.

> 보기 My sister will be back this weekend.
> → My sister **is going to be** back this weekend.

1. I will help him move tomorrow.
    → I _____ him move tomorrow.

2. The store will not open this Sunday.
    → The store _____ this Sunday.

3. They won't lie to you again.
    → They _____ to you again.

4. We will eat chickens for dinner.
    → We _____ chicken for dinner.

D 보기와 같이 의문문으로 바꾸고 대답을 완성하세요.

> 보기 Alice is going to prepare for the exam. (Yes)
> → Q: **Is Alice going to prepare for the exam?**   A: **Yes, she is.**

1. Sandra will give you a hand. (No)
    → Q: _____   A: _____

2. Jim is going to see the dentist. (Yes)
    → Q: _____   A: _____

3. It will be cloudy and windy. (Yes)
    → Q: _____   A: _____

4. They are going to arrive at 9 p.m. (No)
    → Q: _____   A: _____

MUST-HAVE 3

E 주어진 미래 관련 표현을 넣어서 문장을 확장해 보세요.

> 보기 There is a math exam. (will, next Monday)
> → There will be a math exam next Monday.

1. The bus leaves. (be going to, in ten minutes)
   떠나다/출발하다
   → _____

2. It snows. (will, next week)
   → _____

3. Do you take the subway? (be going to, tomorrow)
   지하철
   → _____

4. I don't go swimming. (will, this weekend)
   → _____

F 주어진 단어들을 바르게 배열하여 문장을 완성하세요.(참고: 영어는 항상 '주어'를 먼저 찾아야 해요.)

1. next week / will / call you / I
   → _____
   (나는 다음 주에 너에게 전화할 것이다.)

2. stay in Seoul / He / for two weeks / is going to
   → _____
   (그는 2주 동안 서울에 머무를 것이다.)

3. is going to / in a minute / The doctor / see you
   → _____
   (의사가 곧 당신을 진료할 것이다.)

4. give me / Will / one more chance / you
   → _____
   (내게 기회를 한 번 더 주겠니?)

Unit 02 미래의 조동사

Part 3 Writing Practice

A 주어진 단어들을 활용하여 문장을 영작하세요.

at the party 파티에서	blue 파란색의	dress 드레스	family 가족
go on a trip 여행을 가다	here 여기로	move 옮기다	pink 분홍색의
plant pot 화분	play tennis 테니스를 치다	take 가져가다	take a picture 사진을 찍다
this morning 오늘 아침	tomorrow 내일	umbrella 우산	wear 입다

1. Ken은 오늘 아침에 테니스를 칠 것이다. (be going to)

   → _____

   (Ken은 / 할 것이다 / 테니스를 치다 / 오늘 아침에)

2. Bob은 파티에서 사진을 찍을 것이다. (be going to)

   → _____

   (Bob은 / 할 것이다 / 사진을 찍다 / 파티에서)

3. 나는 이 분홍색 우산을 가져가지 않을 것이다. (will)

   → _____

   (나는 / 않을 것이다 / 가져가다 / 이 분홍색 우산을)

4. 그녀는 내일 파란 드레스를 입을까요? (be going to)

   → _____

   (그녀는 / 할까요 / 입다 / 파란 드레스를 / 내일)

5. 너는 그 화분을 여기로 옮길 거니? (be going to)

   → _____

   (너는 / 할 거니 / 옮기다 / 그 화분을 / 여기로)

6. 그는 그의 가족들과 여행을 갈 것이다. (will)

   → _____

   (그는 / 할 것이다 / 여행을 가다 / 그의 가족과)

MUST-HAVE 3

B 주어진 단어들을 활용하여 단락을 완성하세요.

buy 사다	food 음식	on the weekend 주말에	open 열다
pet shop 애견 용품점	school library 학교도서관	some 약간의	stop by (잠시) 들르다
study 공부하다	together 함께	vet 수의사	

1 The science exam is next week. _____
(우리는 / 할 것이다 (be going to) / 공부하다 / 함께 /

_____. _____.
주말에)　　　　　　　　(학교도서관은 / 않을 것이다 (will) / 열다 /

_____. So we will use the library in the neighborhood.
이번 주말에)　　　　　　　　　　　　　　　　　　　　　　근처/인근/이웃

2 My pet Popo is sick. _____.
(나는 / 할 것이다 (be going to) / 데리고 가다 / 그를 / 수의사에게)

He will get some shots. On the way home, _____
주사들　　도중에/~가는 중에　　　　　　　　(우리는 / 할 것이다 (will) / 들르다 /

_____ for him.
애견 용품점에 / 사기 위해 / 약간의 음식을)

C 그림을 묘사해 보세요.

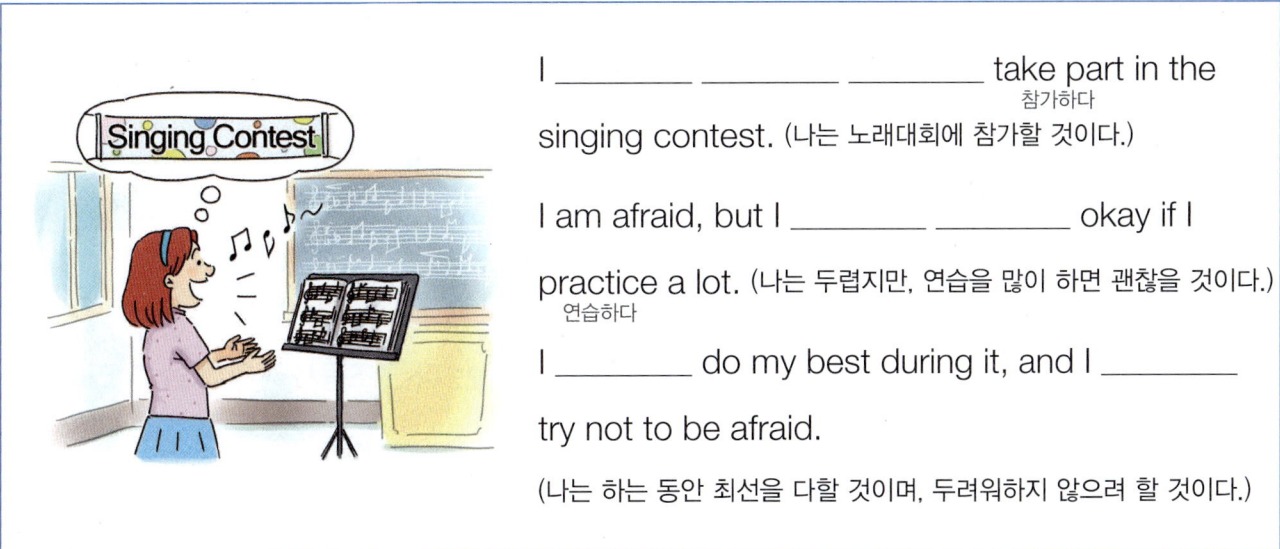

I _____ _____ _____ take part in the
　　　　　　　　　　　　　　참가하다
singing contest. (나는 노래대회에 참가할 것이다.)

I am afraid, but I _____ _____ okay if I

practice a lot. (나는 두렵지만, 연습을 많이 하면 괜찮을 것이다.)
연습하다

I _____ do my best during it, and I _____

try not to be afraid.

(나는 하는 동안 최선을 다할 것이며, 두려워하지 않으려 할 것이다.)

* 주요 어휘는 Word Test p.112에서 한 번 더 연습하세요.

Unit 03 가능·추측·허가의 조동사

Part 1 Grammar Point

A can과 may는 가능성, 추측, 허가를 구할 때 사용하는 조동사입니다.

can	may
가능 ~할 수 있다 I **can** play many musical instruments. 나는 많은 악기를 연주할 수 있다.	**추측** ~일지도 모른다 He **may** know Silvia's phone number. 그는 Silvia의 전화번호를 알지도 모른다.
허가 ~해도 좋다 **Can** I see your student ID? Yes, you **can**. 내가 당신의 학생증을 봐도 될까요? 네, 보세요.	**허가** ~해도 좋다 You **may** take whatever you want. 너는 네가 원하는 것은 무엇이든 가져가도 좋다.
could can의 과거, 희박한 가능성 She **could** attend the school concert. 그녀는 학교 콘서트에 참석할 수 있었다.	**might** may의 과거, 희박한 추측 I **might** stay home, or I **might** go out. 나는 집에 있을 수도 있고, 밖에 나갈지도 모른다.

B be able to는 can보다 더 잘할 수 있는 능력일 때 씁니다.

조동사	부정문	의문문
can	주어 + cannot (can't) + 동사원형	Can + 주어 + 동사원형~?
be able to	주어 + be동사 + not + able to + 동사원형	be동사 + 주어 + able to + 동사원형~?

* be able to는 주어의 인칭과 시제에 맞춰 사용해야 합니다.

- Danny **is able to** write his name.   Danny는 자기 이름을 쓸 수 있다.
  (= can)
- **Was** he **able to** change his schedule?   그는 스케줄을 바꿀 수 있었나요?
  (= Could he)

C can은 다른 조동사와 함께 쓰지 못해요. 하지만 be able to는 다른 조동사와 함께 쓸 수 있어요.

- I will be able to speak English fluently soon.   나는 곧 영어를 유창하게 할 수 있을 것이다.
  will can (x)
- Bobby might be able to come with us.   Bobby는 우리와 함께 갈 수 있을지도 모른다.
  might can (x)

Part 2 Grammar Exercise

A ① 주어진 상황을 가장 잘 설명할 수 있는 조동사와 동사를 고르세요.

| can
~할 수 있다 | save
~살리다 | come in
~안으로 들어오다 | may
~할지도 모른다 | climb up
~(위에)오르다 | be able to
~할 수 있다 |

② A와 B의 대화를 완성하세요.

1
A: _____ you _____ the mountain?
　　　　　　　　　　　　　　　　　　　산
B: Yes, I can.

2
The man will _____ _____ her life.

3
A: _____ I _____?
B: Yes, you may.

B 문법적으로 가장 올바른 조동사를 고르세요.

1 I don't believe the story, but it (might / able to) be true.

2 (May / Can) Nancy speak four languages?

3 I (could / might) not go to the concert last week.

4 Mac is strong. He is (able to / may) carry the box.
　　　　　　　　　　　　　　　　　　　　　나르다/들고 있다

5 I met Sue a long time ago, but I (can / may) have her phone number.
　　　　　　오랜 시간 전

Unit 03 가능·추측·허가의 조동사

C be able to를 사용해서 밑줄 친 내용을 정확하게 표현하세요.

> 보기 She will can pass the exam next year.
> → She will be able to pass the exam next year.

1 They won't can get tickets for the game.
   → They _____ get tickets for the game.

2 You may can find the answer to the question.
      찾다
   → You _____ find the answer to the question.

3 I hurt my leg. I will not can play soccer.
     다쳤다
   → I hurt my leg. I _____ play soccer.

4 Dan will can come home tomorrow.
   → Dan _____ come home tomorrow.

D 주어진 조동사를 사용해서 문장의 뉘앙스를 바꿔보세요.

> 보기 Jay wants you to say hello. (might)
> → Jay might want you to say hello.

1 There are some mistakes in his homework. (could)
   → _____

2 We are able to enjoy the picnic next week. (will)
   → _____

3 That is another chance for you. (may)
       또 하나
   → _____

4 They found the way to the station. (be able to)
          찾았다
   → _____

E 조동사가 사용된 문장을 의문문과 부정문으로 바꿔주세요.

1 Gary is able to write a good essay. (의문문)
   → _____

2 It may be sunny tomorrow morning. (부정문)
   → _____

3 I was able to take the ski class. (부정문)
   → _____

4 She was able to finish her test. (의문문)
       끝내다
   → _____

5 They could arrive here on time. (부정문)
                        정시에
   → _____

F 주어진 단어들을 바르게 배열하여 문장을 완성하세요. (참고: 영어는 항상 '주어'를 먼저 찾아야 해요.)

1 the yellow shirt / try on / I / May
   → _____
   (내가 그 노란 셔츠를 입어봐도 될까요?)

2 how to play chess / might / She / know
   → _____
   (그녀는 체스하는 방법을 알지도 모른다.)

3 get enough sleep / Were you / last night / able to
   → _____
   (어제 밤에 너는 충분히 잘 수 있었니?)

4 after dinner / You / start the game / can
   → _____
   (너는 저녁 식사 후에 게임을 시작해도 좋다.)

Unit 03 가능 · 추측 · 허가의 조동사

Part 3 Writing Practice

A 주어진 단어들을 활용하여 문장을 영작하세요.

answer (전화를) 받다	call 전화	come 오다	dictionary 사전
for a minute 잠깐	help 도움	here 여기에	lose 지다
match 시합	next year 내년에	take a class 수업을 듣다	tomorrow 내일
use 사용하다	walk 걷다	without ~없이	

1 내가 잠깐 너의 사전을 사용해도 될까? (may)

→ _____

(해도 될까 / 내가 / 사용하다 / 너의 사전을 / 잠깐)

2 우리는 시합에 질지도 모른다. (might)

→ _____

(우리는 / 할지도 모른다 / 지다 / 시합에)

3 나는 그의 도움 없이는 걸을 수 없었다. (could)

→ _____

(나는 / 할 수 없었다 / 걷다 / 없이 / 그의 도움)

4 David는 내일은 여기에 올 수 있을 거야.

→ _____

(David는 / 할 수 있을 것이다 / 오다 / 여기에 / 내일은)

5 너는 내년에 수업을 들을 수 있을지도 모른다.

→ _____

(너는 / 할 수 있을지도 모른다 / 수업을 듣다 / 내년에)

6 나는 너의 전화를 받을 수 없었어. (could)

→ _____

(나는 / 할 수 없었다 / 받다 / 너의 전화를)

MUST-HAVE 3

B 주어진 단어들을 활용하여 단락을 완성하세요.

| at first 처음에는 | coach 코치 | do 하다 | easy 쉬운 |
| online shopping 온라인 쇼핑 | store 가게 | weekend 주말 | |

1 _____. But we will
　(그 가게는 / 아닐지도 모른다 / 열다 / 이번 주말에)

be able to buy it some other way. _____.
　　　　　　　　　　　　　　다른 방법으로　　　(우리는 / 할 수 있다 / 온라인 쇼핑을)

Or we may go to a flea market.
　　　　　　　　　벼룩시장

2 I decided to become a swimmer. _____.
　　결심했다　　　　　　　　　　　　(그것은 / 아닐지도 모른다 / 쉽지 / 처음에는)

But _____. Someday,
　　(나는 / 할 수 있다 / 그것을 / 좋은 코치의 도움으로)　　　　언젠가/머지않아

I will be on the national swim team.
　　　　　　　　国가의

C 그림을 묘사해 보세요.

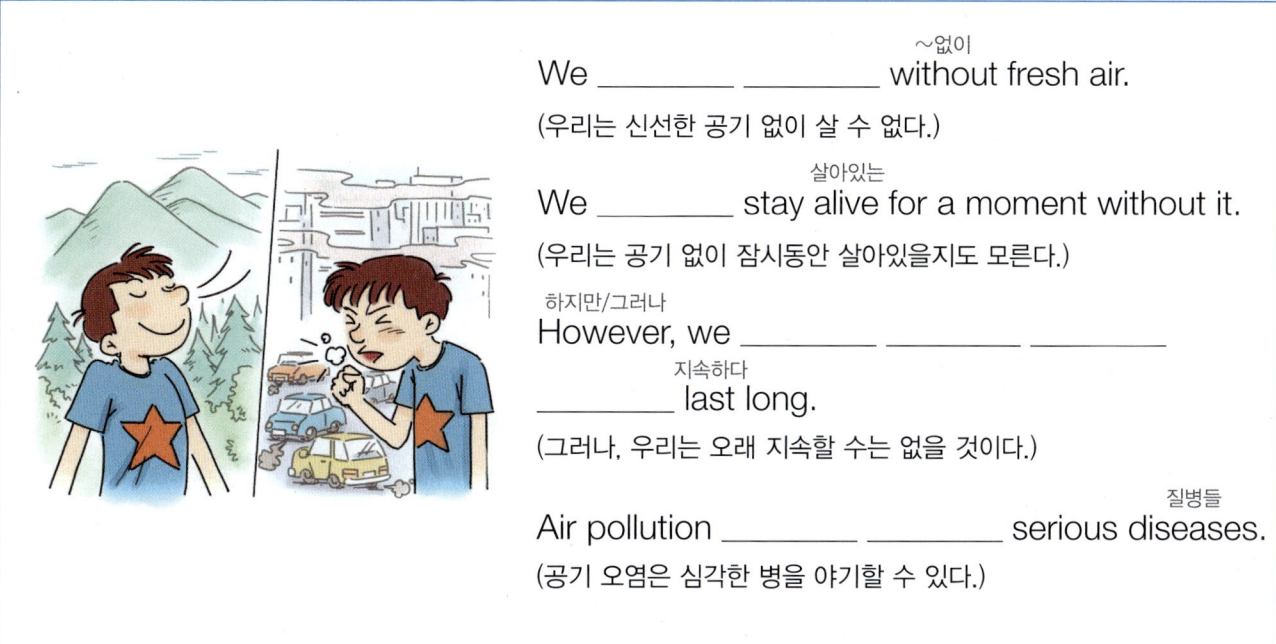

　　　　　　　　　　　　　　　　　~없이
We _____ _____ without fresh air.
(우리는 신선한 공기 없이 살 수 없다.)

　　　　　　　　　　살아있는
We _____ stay alive for a moment without it.
(우리는 공기 없이 잠시동안 살아있을지도 모른다.)

하지만/그러나
However, we _____ _____ _____
　　지속하다
_____ last long.
(그러나, 우리는 오래 지속할 수는 없을 것이다.)

　　　　　　　　　　　　　　질병들
Air pollution _____ _____ serious diseases.
(공기 오염은 심각한 병을 야기할 수 있다.)

* 주요 어휘는 Word Test p.113에서 한 번 더 연습하세요.

Review 01 Journal

A 아래 표를 참고하여, 여름 방학을 계획하는 글에 들어갈 내용을 정리하세요.

Plans	Reasons
take swimming lessons	will take part in a swimming competition 대회
read as many books as possible 가능한	can learn many things from books
do volunteer work 자원봉사	will be helpful in many ways 도움이 되는

OUTLINE

Title   My Summer Vacation Plans

Beginning   made some plans for my summer vacation

Middle
- am going to take swimming lessons
  → _____ take part in a swimming competition
- am _____ _____ read as many books as possible
  → _____ learn many things from books
- will _____ volunteer work
  → might be hard; but will _____ helpful in many ways
  ~일지도 모른다

Ending   will stick to my plans
달라붙다

---

competition 경기   stick to ~에 충실하다(잘 지키다)   take part in ~에 참가하다

B 아웃라인을 바탕으로 여름 방학을 계획하는 글을 완성하세요.

My Summer Vacation Plans — Title

I made _____. — Beginning

First, I _____. I need to
learn swimming because I _____ a swimming
competition.

Second, I _____
_____. I couldn't read books because I didn't have enough
time. I think I _____ from books.

Third, I _____. I am afraid it _____
　　　　　　　　　　　　　　　　　　　　　　　걱정된다
_____ to do. But I believe that it _____
in many ways.

I _____ stick to my plans. — Ending

— Middle

아래 내용을 모두 잘 학습하였으면 □안에 ✔하세요.

☐ 조동사를 내용에 맞게 사용하였다.

☐ 미래를 나타내는 조동사를 맞게 사용하였다.

☐ 가능, 추측, 허가를 나타내는 조동사를 맞게 사용하였다.

Unit 04 의무의 조동사

Part 1 Grammar Point

A must는 '~해야 한다'라는 의미로 강한 의무를 나타내는 조동사입니다.

- You **must** cross the street at the green light. 너는 녹색신호에 길을 건너야 한다.
- You **must** come back to the dorm by midnight. 너는 자정까지 기숙사에 돌아와야 한다.

B have to는 must와 같은 의미로써 has to, had to로 변할 수 있습니다.

시제	형태	예문
현재	**have (has) to** = must ~해야 한다	Bob **has to** turn in his essay by tomorrow. Bob은 내일까지 그의 에세이를 제출해야 한다.
과거	**had to** ~해야 했다	He **had to** get up early yesterday morning. 그는 어제 아침에 일찍 일어나야 했다.
미래	**will have to** ~해야 할 것이다	She **will have to** clean her room by herself. 그녀는 혼자 자신의 방을 치워야 할 것이다.

C should는 '~하는 것이 좋다' 혹은 '(마땅히) ~해야 한다'의 의미로 조언을 하거나 당연한 것을 말할 때 사용해요.

- You **should** work out to stay in shape. 너는 건강한 몸을 유지하기 위해 운동을 하는 것이 좋다.
- You **should** not be late for the interview. 너는 면접에 늦으면 안 된다.

* must, have to, should 모두 '~해야 합니다'의 의미로 쓰이지만, 그 강도는 <u>must > have to > should</u>의 순서입니다.

D must not, should not이 들어가면 부정문이 만들어집니다. have to의 부정문은 don't have to로 쓰면 돼요.

조동사	부정문	의문문
must	주어 + must not + 동사원형	Must + 주어 + 동사원형~?
have to	주어 + don't / doesn't / didn't + have to + 동사원형	Do / Does / Did + 주어 + have to + 동사원형~?
should	주어 + should not + 동사원형	Should + 주어 + 동사원형~?

* must not은 '~해서는 안 된다'의 <u>금지</u>를 의미하고, don't have to 는 '~할 필요가 없다'는 <u>불필요</u>를 나타냅니다.

Part 2 Grammar Exercise

A ① 주어진 상황을 가장 잘 설명할 수 있는 조동사와 동사를 찾으세요.

have to	must not	should	park	fix	apologize
~(반드시)해야 한다	~해서는 안되다 (강한금지)	~해야 한다	주차하다	고치다	사과하다

② 자연스러운 내용이 되도록 문장을 완성하세요.

1  She will _____ _____ the oven as soon as possible.
곧/빨리

2  You _____ _____ when you do something wrong.

3  He _____ _____ in front of the building.
~의 앞에

B 주어의 인칭에 따라서 have to를 쓸지, has to를 쓸지 정해야 합니다. 올바른 have to, has to를 정하세요.

1 My sister (have to / has to) take a ballet class after school.

2 I (have to / has to) save money to buy a gift for Mother's Day.
저축하다

3 Do you (have to / has to) stop by the convenience store?
편의점

4 People are studying. We (have to / has to) be quiet at the library.
조용한

5 Jim is sick. He (have to / has to) go to the hospital.
아픈

Unit 04 의무의 조동사

C 가장 알맞은 조동사 표현을 골라 문장을 완성하세요.

| doesn't have to
~할 필요가 없다 | must not
~해서는 안 된다
(강한 금지) | don't have to
~할 필요가 없다 | should
~해야 한다 |

1 We have enough time. You _____ hurry.

2 We _____ speak loudly at night.

3 She _____ cook the food. The party is over.
  끝이 난

4 You _____ see a doctor. You have a very high fever.
  열

D 주어진 시제를 살려서 must(강한 금지)를 have to로 바꾸면서 그 강도를 낮춰보세요.

> 보기 I must send Susan an important message right now. (현재)
> → I have to send Susan an important message right now.

1 He must cancel his appointment with the doctor. (과거)
  약속
  → _____

2 They must stop by the gas station soon. (미래)
  잠시 들리다   주유소
  → _____

3 Andy must finish his speech within five minutes. (현재)
  ~안에
  → _____

4 She must help her brother care for his son. (과거)
  돌봐주다
  → _____

E 조동사가 사용된 문장을 의문문 또는 부정문으로 바꿔주세요.

1. She had to eat a late-night snack. (부정문)
   → _____

2. They should stop smoking. (의문문)
   → _____

3. Randy must do the dishes for Mom. (의문문)
   → _____

4. He has to fly to New York tomorrow. (부정문)
   → _____

F 주어진 단어들을 바르게 배열하여 문장을 완성하세요.(참고: 영어는 항상 '주어'를 먼저 찾아야 해요.)

1. worry / You / about your future / don't have to
   → _____
   (너는 너의 미래에 대해 걱정할 필요가 없다.)

2. about the secret / should not / We / tell anyone
   → _____
   (우리는 그 비밀에 대해 아무에게도 얘기해서는 안 된다.)

3. to children / must not / People / use bad words
   → _____
   (사람들은 아이들에게 나쁜 말을 쓰면 안 된다.)

4. tomorrow / bring / Should I / my student ID
   → _____
   (내가 내일 학생증을 가져와야 하나요?)

Unit 04 의무의 조동사

Part 3 Writing Practice

A 주어진 단어들을 활용하여 문장을 영작하세요.

area 지역	breakfast 아침 식사	break one's promise 약속을 어기다
catch (탈 것을) 타다	change 바꾸다	do one's best 최선을 다하다
everything 모든 것	mind 마음	ride 타다
skateboard 스케이트보드	skip 거르다	wait 기다리다

1 너는 약속을 어기면 안 된다. (should)

→ _____
(너는 / 하면 안 된다 / 약속을 어기다)

2 너는 10분 동안 기다려야 할 것이다.

→ _____
(너는 / 해야 할 것이다 / 기다리다 / 10분 동안)

3 우리는 우리 마음을 바꿀 필요가 없다.

→ _____
(우리는 / 할 필요가 없다 / 바꾸다 / 우리 마음을)

4 그들은 이 지역에서 스케이트보드를 타서는 안 된다. (must)

→ _____
(그들은 / 하면 안 된다 / (자신들의) 스케이트보드를 타다 / 이 지역에서)

5 그녀는 그 버스를 타기 위해 아침을 걸러야만 했다. (have to)

→ _____
(그녀는 / 해야 했다 / 아침을 거르다 / 그 버스를 타기 위해)

6 너는 모든 것에 있어서 최선을 다해야 한다. (should)

→ _____
(너는 / 해야 한다 / 너의 최선을 다하다 / 모든 것에 있어서)

MUST-HAVE 3

B 주어진 단어들을 활용하여 단락을 완성하세요.

> because of 때문에   keep regular hours 규칙적인 생활을 하다   move 이사하다
> take a long walk 오래 걷다   take a nap 낮잠을 자다

1 A: I stayed up all night again. I am very tired now.
　　　　안 자다/깨어있다　　　　　　　　　　피곤한

　　B: _____.
　　　(너는 / 하는 것이 좋겠다 (should) / 집에 가다 / 그리고 / 낮잠을 자다)

　　A: You're right. I think _____.
　　　　　　　　　　　　　　　(나는 / 해야 한다 (must) / 규칙적인 생활을 하다)

2 Jamie moved to this town a year ago. _____
　　　　　　　이사했다　　　　　　　　　　　(그는 / 해야 했다 (have to) / 이사하다 / 여기로 /

_____. Now, _____
　　때문에 / 그의 학교)　　　　　　　　　　　　(그는 / 할 필요가 없다 /

_____.
　　오래 걷다 / 학교까지)

C 그림을 묘사해 보세요.

A: Do you _____ _____ _____ now?
　　(너는 지금 떠나야 하니?)

B: Yes, I _____ _____ there before three.
　　(응, 세 시 전에 (반드시) 거기에 도착해야 해.)

A: OKay, but you _____ _____ _____
　　　　　　　　　　　　　　　　　걸리다
_____. It only takes an hour.
　(좋아, 하지만 서두를 필요는 없어. 한 시간 밖에 안 걸려.)

＊ 주요 어휘는 Word Test p.113에서 한 번 더 연습하세요.

Unit 05 습관의 조동사

Part 1 Grammar Point

A used to와 would는 과거의 습관이나 상태를 나타내는 조동사입니다.

조동사	의 미	예 문
used to	~하곤 했다	• Charlie **used to** go camping every summer. Charlie는 여름마다 캠핑을 가곤 했다. • I **used to** go fishing with my father. 나는 아버지와 낚시를 가곤 했다.
used to	~이었다 (과거의 상태)	• My mom **used to** be an English teacher. 나의 엄마는 영어 선생님이었다. (지금은 영어 선생님이 아님) • Our city **used to** be a small town. 우리 도시는 작은 마을이었다. (지금은 작은 마을이 아님)
would	~하곤 했다	• They **would** visit me quite often. 그들은 나를 꽤 자주 방문하곤 했다. • When he was young, he **would** play tennis. 그가 젊었을 때는 테니스를 치곤 했다.

B would는 '~하고 싶다'라고 공손하게 요청이나 제안을 할 때 사용하면 됩니다. 또는, '차라리~하는 것이 낫다'라고 말할 때 사용하세요.

조동사	의 미	예 문
would like to	~하고 싶다 (공손한 요청이나 제안)	• I **would like to** take a walk in the park. 나는 공원에서 산책을 하고 싶다. • **Would** you **like to** have sandwich for lunch? 당신은 점심으로 샌드위치를 먹고 싶습니까?
would rather	차라리 ~하는 것이 낫다	• I **would rather** go alone. 나는 차라리 혼자 가는 것이 낫겠다. • I **would rather** order chicken than pizza. 나는 피자보다는 차라리 치킨을 주문하겠다.

Part 2 Grammar Exercise

A ① 내용상 알맞는 조동사와 동사를 고르세요.

would	would rather	used to	take care of	be	take
~하곤 했다 (불규칙적)	차라리~하겠다	~하곤 했다 (규칙적)	~를 돌보다	~이 되다	(교통수단)타다

② 주어진 상황을 완성하세요.

1  She _____ _____ a famous movie star.

2  My grandfather _____ _____ me when my parents were busy.
바쁜

3  I _____ _____ the bus than walk alone.

B 해석상 가장 어울리는 조동사 표현을 고르세요.

1 She is very bright. But she (would / used to) be shy.
　똑똑한　　　　　　　　　　　　　　　　　부끄러움을 많이 타는

2 There (would / used to) be a tall building near my house.
　　　　　　　　　　　　　　　　　　　　~근처에

3 Tom (would / would rather) go hiking when he was young.

4 They (used to / would like to) go to church when they lived in Korea.

5 I (would rather / would like to) see a doctor than be sick all day.

Unit 05 습관의 조동사

C 적절한 조동사 표현을 골라 두 문장이 같은 뜻이 되도록 만드세요.

would	would like to	would rather	used to

1. I want to have a hamburger for lunch.
   → I _____ have a hamburger for lunch.

2. I like going to a movie with Cindy more than Bob.
   → I _____ go to a movie with Cindy than Bob.

3. I didn't drink a lot of milk. Now, I drink it a lot.
   → I _____ not drink a lot of milk.

4. There was a lake in my hometown. Now, there is no lake.
   호수
   → There _____ be a lake in my hometown.

D 주어진 조동사를 사용해서 문장의 뉘앙스를 바꿔주세요.

> 보기 Doris had a cute dog as a pet. (used to)
> → Doris used to have a cute dog as a pet.

1. Gary was a film director. (used to)
   영화   감독
   → _____

2. I stay poor than steal things. (would rather)
   훔치다
   → _____

3. I make an appointment with Dr. Smith. (would like to)
   → _____

4. The restaurant serves traditional food. (would)
   전통적인
   → _____

E would like to 또는 would rather를 사용하여 두 문장이 최대한 같은 뜻이 되도록 만드세요.

> 보기 I want to climb up the tall tree.
> → I would like to climb up the tall tree.

1 I want to be a famous actor.
   유명한
   → _____

2 She prefers to stay home alone.
   ~을 더 좋아한다
   → _____

3 I want to buy those small toys.
   → _____

4 We prefer to play hide-and-seek on the playground.
   숨바꼭질   운동장/놀이터
   → _____

F 주어진 단어들을 바르게 배열하여 문장을 완성하세요.(참고: 영어는 항상 '주어'를 먼저 찾아야 해요.)

1 after a game / would drink / He / a lot of water
   → _____
   (그는 경기 후에 많은 물을 마시곤 했다.)

2 when she was young / used to / Jane / be shy
   → _____
   (Jane은 어렸을 때 수줍음이 많았다.)

3 would rather / than order in / eat out / We
                  주문하다
   → _____
   (우리는 음식을 배달시키는 것보다 차라리 외식하는 게 낫겠다.)

4 live / like to / Would you / in the countryside
   → _____
   (당신은 시골에서 살고 싶습니까?)

Unit 05 습관의 조동사

Part 3 Writing Practice

A 주어진 단어들을 활용하여 문장을 영작하세요.

after 후에	a long time ago 오래 전에는	clean 깨끗한	drink 마시다
every time 매번	go hiking 등산하러 가다	lake 호수	lunch 점심
orange juice 오렌지 주스	own 자신의	sometimes 가끔씩	stay (그대로) 있다
take a walk 산책하다			

1 그는 자신의 차를 가지고 있었다. (지금은 차가 없음)

   → _____
   (그는 / 이었다 / 가지다 / 자신의(그의) 차를)

2 그들은 가끔씩 등산을 가곤 했다. (would)

   → _____
   (그들은 / 하곤 했다 / 가끔씩 / 등산을 가다)

3 그 호수는 오래 전에는 깨끗했었다. (지금은 깨끗하지 않음)

   → _____
   (그 호수는 / 이었다 / 깨끗하다 / 오래 전에는)

4 밖에 비가 온다. 나는 차라리 집에 있는 것이 낫겠다.

   → It is raining outside. _____
   (나는 / 차라리 ~하는 것이 낫다 / (그대로) 있다 / 집에)

5 나는 오렌지 주스를 마시고 싶다.

   → _____
   (나는 / 하고 싶다 / 마시다 / 오렌지 주스를)

6 그는 점심 후에 매번 산책을 하곤 했다. (used to)

   → _____
   (그는 / 하곤 했다 / 산책하다 / 점심 후에 / 매번)

MUST-HAVE 3

B 주어진 단어들을 활용하여 단락을 완성하세요.

a lot 많이	computer game 컴퓨터 게임	every day 매일	famous 유명한
hour 시간	in the water 물 속에서	more than ~보다 더	play (게임을) 하다
practice 연습하다	soccer 축구	swimmer 수영선수	

1 _____. _____
(나는 / 이었다 / 유명한 수영선수) (지금은 아님)   (나는 /

_____. Now, I don't go
하곤 했다 (used to) / 연습하다 / 많이 / 물 속에서 / 매일)

swimming often. I'd rather play tennis than go swimming.
　　　　　　　　차라리~하겠다

2 _____. He doesn't play
(Jack은 / 하곤 했다 (would) / 컴퓨터 게임을 / 2시간 보다 더)

them long now. He tries to spend time outdoors. _____
　　　　　　　　보내다　　　　옥외의/야외의　　　　(그는 / 차라리 ~ 하는 것이 낫다 /

_____.
축구를 하다 / 보다는 / 컴퓨터 게임을 하다)

C 그림을 묘사해 보세요.

There _____ _____ _____ a big tree in front of his house. (그의 집 앞에는 큰 나무가 있었다.)

He _____ often _____ up the tree.
　　　　　　　　　　　~위에
(그는 자주 그 나무에 오르곤 했다.)

And he _____ sometimes _____ books under the tree.
　~아래에
(그리고 그는 가끔 그 나무 밑에서 책을 읽곤 했다.)

* 주요 어휘는 Word Test p.114에서 한 번 더 연습하세요.

Unit 06 부사절을 만드는 접속사 1

Part 1 Grammar Point

A 문장을 [절]이라고 합니다. 이 [절]앞에 [부사접속사]를 쓰면 [부사절]이 만들어집니다.
외우기 쉽게 순서를 정하면 [부사접속사(when, after...) + 주어 + 동사]가 됩니다.

앞, 뒤 내용을 연결해주는 접속사		의미	예문
시 간	when	~할 때	I usually listen to music **when** I study. 나는 공부할 때 주로 음악을 듣는다.
	after	~한 후에	She will have dinner **after** she finishes her homework. 그녀는 숙제를 끝낸 후에 저녁을 먹을 것이다.
	before	~하기 전에	**Before** I go to bed, I brush my teeth. 나는 잠자리에 들기 전에 이를 닦는다.
	until	~할 때까지	You have to wait here **until** he comes back. 너는 그가 돌아올 때까지 여기서 기다려야 한다.
이 유	because	~때문에	All the shops were closed **because** it was a holiday. 휴일이었기 때문에 모든 상점들이 문을 닫았다.

* 부사접속사 종류는 Appendix p.110 참고

B 시제는 주절과 부사절을 동일하게 맞춰주는 것이 일반적입니다. 그러나 미래를 나타내는 경우 부사절에는 will을 쓰지 않고 현재형으로 미래의 의미를 대신해요.

주절 + 부사절	예문
현재 + 현재	They often **go** to an outlet store when they **go** shopping. 그들은 쇼핑을 가면 종종 아울렛 매장으로 간다.
과거 + 과거	I **went** home after her flight **left**. 나는 그녀의 비행기가 떠나고 나서 집으로 갔다.
미래 + 현재	She **will** stay in the hospital until she **gets** well. 그녀는 건강이 좋아질 때까지 병원에 머물 것이다.

Part 2 Grammar Exercise

A 주어진 상황을 설명하기 위해서 가장 적절한 접속사를 골라 문장을 완성하세요.

when	after	until
~할 때	~후에	~할 때까지

1. I like singing. I am happy _____ I sing.

2. _____ I worked out, I took a shower.
   운동하다

3. I will wait inside the building _____ the rain stops.

B 내용상 가장 적절한 접속사를 고르세요.

1. I want to study French (before / until) I am fluent.
   유창한

2. We didn't go out (because / before) it was too cold.

3. (After / Before) you go out, take an umbrella.
   가져가다

4. My dad cleaned the room (until / after) he washed the dishes.

5. (When / Before) I saw Paul, I asked him about the lecture.
   강의

Unit 06 부사절을 만드는 접속사 1

C 다음 두 절이 자연스런 내용이 되도록 연결하세요.

1 Her family moved to a city ·   · after I graduate.
   이사갔다

2 You should wait here ·   · when she was five.

3 It started snowing ·   · when I left home.
                                                                                                        떠났다

4 I will get a job ·   · because the road was too muddy.
   얻다/찾다   흙탕물의

5 It was difficult to drive ·   · until I come back.
   어려운

D 어떤 접속사를 사용하는지에 따라서 내용이 달라집니다. 가장 자연스러운 접속사를 골라 문장을 완성하세요.

after	because	before	until	when
~후에	~때문에	~전에	~할 때까지	~할 때

1 He left the house _____ I woke up. I couldn't say goodbye.
                                                                     일어났다

2 They studied at the library _____ it closed.

3 _____ you called me, I was asleep. Sorry I missed it.
                                                                                  자고있는   놓쳤다

4 She was absent yesterday _____ she had a bad cold.
                  결석한

5 I went outside _____ I put on my coat.
                                     걸치다/입다

MUST-HAVE 3

E 밑줄 친 부분을 고치면 좀더 정확한 내용을 전달할 수 있습니다. 시제를 참고해서 고쳐주세요.

1. Ian practiced many math exercises before the test <u>begins</u>.
   → Ian practiced many math exercises before the test _____.

2. She left the hall before the lecture <u>end</u>.
   홀/회관   끝나다/마치다
   → She left the hall before the lecture _____.

3. I will call you when I <u>will get</u> home.
   이르다/도착하다
   → I will call you when I _____ home.

4. He will go out after the rain <u>will stop</u>.
   → He will go out after the rain _____.

F 주어진 단어들을 바르게 배열하여 문장을 완성하세요.(참고: 영어는 항상 '주어'를 먼저 찾아야 해요.)

1. spring came, / began to bloom / When / flowers
   봄   꽃이 피다
   → _____
   (봄이 왔을 때 꽃들이 피기 시작했다.)

2. I never saw him / Fred / moved to a city, / After
   → _____
   (Fred가 도시로 이사간 후 나는 그를 전혀 보지 못했다.)

3. near there / Jane moved there / because / her sister lived
   → _____
   (Jane은 그녀의 여동생이 근처에 살았기 때문에 거기로 이사 갔다.)

4. I didn't go to sleep / my dad / until / came home
   → _____
   (나는 아빠가 집에 오실 때까지 잠자리에 들지 않았다.)

Unit 06 부사절을 만드는 접속사 1

Part 3 Writing Practice

A 주어진 단어들을 활용하여 문장을 영작하세요.

all right 괜찮은	busy 바쁜	dinner 저녁 식사	downstairs 아래층으로
everything 모든 것	find 발견하다	ready 준비된	say 말하다
something 무언가	take a shower 샤워를 하다	think 생각하다	too much 너무 많이
wake up (잠을) 깨다	watch 보다	with ~와 함께	wrong 잘못된

1 Mike는 그의 엄마가 바쁘기 때문에 엄마를 도왔다.

→ _____

(Mike는 / 도왔다 / (그의) 엄마를 / 때문에 / 그녀가 / 바쁘다)

2 나는 모든 것이 괜찮아질 때까지 너와 함께 있을 것이다.

→ _____

(나는 / 있을 것이다 / 너와 함께 / 때까지 / 모든 것이 / 괜찮다)

3 내가 깨어났을 때 나는 잘못된 무언가를 발견했다.

→ _____

(할 때 / 내가 / 깨어났다 / 나는 / 발견했다 / 무언가를 / 잘못된)

4 Betty는 무언가를 말하기 전에 너무 많이 생각한다.

→ _____

(Betty는 / 생각한다 / 너무 많이 / 전에 / 그녀가 / 말하다 / 무언가를)

5 너는 저녁이 준비될 때까지 TV를 봐도 된다.

→ _____

(너는 / 봐도 된다 / TV를 / 때까지 / 저녁이 준비되다)

6 나는 샤워를 한 후에 아래층으로 내려왔다.

→ _____

(나는 / 왔다 / 아래층으로 / 후에 / 나는 / 샤워를 했다)

MUST-HAVE 3

B 주어진 단어들을 활용하여 단락을 완성하세요.

| go to sleep 잠자리에 들다 | in the play 연극에서 | leading role 주인공 역할 |
| perform 연기하다 | try hard 열심히 하다 | win 이기다, 차지하다 |

1 My brother has a midterm exam next week. He is very busy studying these
   　　　　　　　　　　　　　중간고사　　　　　　　　　　　　　　　　　　　　　　　　　요즘에는

   days. _____. _____
         (그는 / 집에 왔다 / 후에 / 내가 / 잠자리에 들었다)　　　　　(할 때 /

   _____.
   내가 / 깨어났다 / 오늘 아침에 / 그는 / 없었다 / 집에)

2 John is a stage actor. He had an audition yesterday. _____
                                                        (그는 / 열심히 했다 / 때문에 /

   _____. _____
   그는 / 원했다 / 연기하기를 / 그 연극에서)　　(그는 / 행복했다 / 할 때 /

   _____.
   그가 / 주인공 역할을 차지했다)

C 그림을 묘사해 보세요.

_____ I was young, I _____ exercise often.
(나는 어렸을 때는 자주 운동을 하지 않았다.)

However, I _____ to work out regularly
　　　　　　　　　　　　　　　　　　　　규칙적으로
_____ I got sick.
(하지만 나는 아픈 이후로 운동을 규칙적으로 하기로 결심했다.)

These days, I often _____ with my dad
　　요즘
_____ he also needs to do it.
(요즘 아빠도 운동이 필요하기 때문에 나는 아빠와 운동을 자주 한다.)

* 주요 어휘는 Word Test p.114에서 한 번 더 연습하세요.

Review 02 Journal

A 아래 표를 참고하여, 올해 중학생이 되는 Cindy가 작성한 새 학기를 다짐하는 글에 들어갈 내용을 정리하세요.

Promises	Past	Reasons
should get up at 7	used to get up at 8	middle school begins at 8
must do my homework before I do other things	would play computer games; would sometimes forget to do my homework	want to get good grades

OUTLINE

Title Promises to Myself
약속들   나 자신

Beginning become a middle school student, I should make some promises to myself

Middle **Promise 1:** - _____ get up at 7
일어나다

- _____ _____ get up at 8

- middle school begins at 8

Promise 2: - _____ do my homework _____ I do other things

- _____ play computer games after I came back home; _____ sometimes forget to do my homework

- want to get good grades

Ending will keep my promises
지키다

B 아웃라인을 바탕으로 Cindy가 새 학기를 다짐하는 글을 완성하세요.

Promises to Myself — Title

Now that I have become a middle school student, I _____
_____. — Beginning

First, I think I _____. I _____
_____. I heard _____,
so I should get up earlier than before.
                        더 일찍

Second, I think I _____
_____. I _____ after I

came back home. I _____.

I must do my homework because I want to get good grades at

school. — Middle

I will keep my promises. — Ending

✏️ 아래 내용을 모두 잘 학습하였으면 □안에 ✔하세요.

☐ 의무를 나타내는 조동사를 맞게 사용하였다.

☐ 습관을 나타내는 조동사를 맞게 사용하였다.

☐ 부사절을 만드는 접속사를 맞게 사용하였다.

Unit 07 부사절을 만드는 접속사 2

Part 1 Grammar Point

A as long as는 '~하는 한'의 조건의 의미를 가지는 접속사입니다.

- **As long as** you are with me, I can do anything.
  네가 나와 함께 있는 한, 나는 뭐든 할 수 있다.

- **As long as** the weather is good, we will go on a picnic.
  날씨가 좋은 한, 우리는 소풍 갈 것이다.

B even though, even if, although, though는 '비록 ~이지만'의 양보의 의미를 가지는 접속사입니다.

- **Even though** I was tired, I got up early.
  나는 비록 피곤했지만, 일찍 일어났다.

- **Even if** Sam is 100 years old, he is very healthy.
  Sam은 100세이지만, 그는 매우 건강하다.

- **Although** Nancy made a mistake, I didn't blame her.
  Nancy가 비록 실수를 했지만, 나는 그녀를 탓하지 않았다.

- **Though** she has never been to America, she speaks English well.
  그녀는 전혀 미국에 가본 적이 없지만, 영어를 잘한다.

C as soon as는 '~하자마자'의 시간의 의미를 가지는 접속사입니다.

- **As soon as** he saw me, he ran away.
  그는 나를 보자마자, 도망쳤다.

- I started studying **as soon as** I got up.
  나는 일어나자마자 공부를 시작하였다.

* as long as(조건), even though(양보), as soon as(시간)는 모두 부사절을 이끄는 접속사이므로 뒤에는 절(주어 + 동사)이 옵니다. Unit 6에서 배운 대로 부사절에는 미래의 will을 쓰지 않습니다.

Part 2 Grammar Exercise

A 주어진 상황과 가장 잘 어울리는 접속사를 골라 문장을 완성하세요.

as long as	even though	as soon as
~하는 한	비록~이지만	~하자마자(곧)

1. _____ we are here, we are safe.
   안전한

2. _____ I arrived, the bus left.

3. _____ it is snowing, we will go out.

B 내용상 가장 올바른 접속사를 고르세요.

1 (As long as / As soon as) he came back, everybody cheered.
  환호했다

2 (As soon as / Even though) James is very young, he is polite.
  예의바른

3 I will be his friend (as long as / as soon as) he is a good person.

4 (Even though / As long as) it is April, it is still cold.

5 Joanne spread the news (even though / as soon as) she heard it.
  퍼뜨리다   들었다

Unit 07 부사절을 만드는 접속사 2

C 다음 두 절이 자연스러운 내용이 되도록 연결하세요.

1 You can keep it • • even if he is tired.
   가지다/유지하다

2 I stopped the car • • even though it was new.
   비록~이지만

3 He should practice hard • • as soon as I saw the boy.

4 The printer broke down • • as long as it doesn't rain.
   고장났다

5 We will go to the beach • • as long as you need it.

D 해석이 어색하지 않도록 가장 자연스러운 접속사를 골라 문장을 완성하세요. (중복사용가능)

even though	as long as	as soon as
비록~이지만	~하는 한	~하자마자

1 I opened the window _____ I got home.

2 I won't give up _____ there is a chance.
   포기하다   기회

3 She didn't pass the exam _____ she was smart.

4 He likes any cities _____ they have mountains.

5 We went for a walk _____ the weather was bad.
   산책했다

MUST-HAVE 3

E 시제를 정확하게 쓰면 내용도 정확해집니다. 밑줄 친 부분의 시제를 고치세요.

1. As soon as I come home, I <u>washed</u> my hands.
   → As soon as I come home, I _____ my hands.

2. I turned in the report even though it <u>is</u> a little late.
   → I turned in the report even though it _____ a little late.

3. He will buy the machine as long as it <u>will work</u> well.
   → He will buy the machine as long as it _____ well.

4. As long as you <u>will be</u> on my team, you should follow my instructions.
   → As long as you _____ on my team, you should follow my instructions.

F 주어진 단어들을 바르게 배열하여 문장을 완성하세요.(참고: 영어는 항상 '주어'를 먼저 찾아야 해요.)

1. too / you are okay, / I am fine, / As long as
   → _____
   (네가 괜찮으면, 나도 괜찮다.)

2. pretty strong / Even though / he is / Jake is thin,
   → _____
   (Jake는 말랐지만, 꽤 튼튼하다.)

3. began to rain / As soon as / we arrived home, / it
   → _____
   (우리가 집에 도착하자 마자, 비가 오기 시작했다.)

4. I will arrive at school / on time / As long as / the bus is not late,
   → _____
   (버스가 늦지 않는 한, 나는 학교에 제시간에 도착할 것이다.)

Unit 07 부사절을 만드는 접속사 2

Part 3 Writing Practice

A 주어진 단어들을 활용하여 문장을 영작하세요.

cold 추운	drawing 그림	expensive 비싼	feel better 상태가 나아지다
friend 친구	go swimming 수영하러 가다	happy 행복한	here 여기에
keep 계속하다	keep quiet 조용히 하다	stay 머무르다	take medicine 약을 먹다
very 매우	volunteer 자원봉사하다	weather 날씨	wonderful 훌륭한

1 비록 날씨는 추웠지만, 그녀는 수영하러 갔다.

→ _____

(비록 ~이지만 / 날씨는 / 추웠다 / 그녀는 / 수영하러 갔다)

2 당신은 친구가 있는 한 행복하다.

→ _____

(하는 한 / 당신은 / 친구가 있다 / (당신은) / 행복하다)

3 그는 약을 먹자마자 상태가 나아졌다.

→ _____

(하자마자 / 그는 / (약간의) 약을 먹었다 / (그는) / 상태가 나아졌다)

4 시간이 있는 한 나는 자원봉사를 계속할 것이다.

→ _____

(나는 / 계속할 것이다 / 자원봉사를 / 하는 한 / (내가) 시간이 있다)

5 그 그림은 훌륭하지 않았음에도 불구하고 매우 비쌌다.

→ _____

(그 그림은 / 매우 비쌌다 / 그럼에도 불구하고 / (그것은) / 훌륭하지 않았다)

6 너는 조용히 하고 있는 한 여기에 머물러도 된다.

→ _____

(너는 / 머물러도 된다 / 여기에 / 하는 한 / (네가) 조용히 하다)

MUST-HAVE 3

B 주어진 단어들을 활용하여 단락을 완성하세요.

> become clear (날이) 맑아지다   continue 계속하다   do one's best 최선을 다하다
> get injured 부상을 입다   journey 여행   play (경기를) 하다
> snow 눈이 내리다   stop 멈추다

1. Jay had a minor injury a week ago. _____
   경미한 부상   (그는 / 할 것이다 / 경기를 하다 /

   _____. _____
   그럼에도 불구하고 / 그는 / 부상을 입었다)   (하는 한 / 그는 / 할 수 있다 / 경기를 하다 /

   _____.
   그는 / 할 것이다 / 최선을 다하다)

2. Ted and his team are stopping climbing because of the bad weather. _____
   등산/등반   (하자마자 /

   _____.
   눈이 멈추다 / 그들은 / 계속할 것이다 / 그들의 여행을)

   Hopefully, _____, they will leave for the summit.
   희망하기를   (하자마자 / 날씨가 / 맑아지다)   ~로 떠나다   산 정상

C 그림을 묘사해 보세요.

Last year, my American friend came to visit Korea. (작년에 나의 미국인 친구가 한국을 방문하러 왔다.)

_____ _____ my English was not perfect,
                                            완벽한
I could talk with him.
(나의 영어실력이 완벽한 것은 아니었지만, 그와 대화할 수 있었다.)

_____ _____ _____ we tried to
         서로/각자   소통하다
understand each other, we could communicate.
(우리가 서로 이해하려고 노력하는 한, 의사소통할 수 있었다.)

* 주요 어휘는 Word Test p.115에서 한 번 더 연습하세요.

Unit 08 수여동사

Part 1 Grammar Point

A 수여동사는 '누구에게 무엇을 주는 것'과 관련이 있는 동사이며, 간접목적어(누구에게)와 직접목적어(무엇을)를 가집니다.

수여동사	예 문	
buy	Mom will **buy** <u>me</u> <u>a fur coat</u>. 　　　　　　간목　　직목	엄마는 내게 털 코트를 사줄 것이다.
give	He **gave** <u>me</u> <u>beautiful flowers</u>. 　　　　간목　　　직목	그는 내게 아름다운 꽃을 주었다.
make	Laura **made** <u>her daughter</u> <u>cookies</u>. 　　　　　　　간목　　　직목	Laura는 딸에게 쿠키를 만들어주었다.
send	Tom **sent** <u>me</u> <u>a nice present</u>. 　　　　간목　　　직목	Tom은 내게 좋은 선물을 보냈다.

B 수여동사는 [간접목적어 + 직접목적어]의 순서로 쓰지만, 전치사를 사용하여 [직접목적어 + 전치사(to/for) + 간접목적어]의 순으로 바꿔 쓸 수 있습니다.

> 주어 + 수여동사 + **간목**(~에게) + **직목**(~을)
>
> = 주어 + 수여동사 + **직목**(~을) + **전치사**(to/for) + **간목**(~에게)

- The website will send you a new ID.　　그 웹사이트는 너에게 새로운 아이디를 보낼 것이다.
  = The website will send a new ID **to** you.
- My mother made me a birthday cake.　　나의 엄마는 내게 생일케이크를 만들어주었다.
  = My mother made a birthday cake **for** me.

＊ to를 쓰는 수여동사: bring, give, lend, send, show, teach, read, write 등
　for를 쓰는 수여동사: build, buy, cook, find, get, make 등

Part 2 Grammar Exercise

A ① 내용상 가장 적절한 수여동사를 고르세요.

send	give	buy
보내주다	주다	사주다

② 시제에 맞게 고쳐 내용을 완성하세요.

1. The school _____ all the students small calendars yesterday.
   달력들

2. Tina _____ Mike a text message this morning.
   문자

3. Dad _____ me something cold to drink last night.

B 간접목적어와 직접목적어의 순서가 올바른 것을 고르세요.

1. He bought (many books me / me many books).
   샀다

2. Kevin sent (us some books / some books us) yesterday.
   보냈다

3. I will show (you beautiful scenery / beautiful scenery you).

4. Randy lent (his notebook me / me his notebook).
   빌려주었다

5. Jean gave (a sweater him / him a sweater).

Unit 08 수여동사

C 내용이 자연스러워지도록 ① ② ③ 순서를 정하세요.

> 보기 Pam some pictures showed me of her.
>   (③)   (①)   (②)

1 The teacher us taught the structure of the Earth.
      ( ) ( )   ( )

2 Did you buy for a gift card Lucy?
           ( ) ( )   ( )

3 My mother for beautiful dresses us made.
         ( )   ( )   ( ) ( )

4 I sent a letter my parents to yesterday.
     ( )   ( )   ( )   ( )

D 주어진 전치사를 사용해서 두 문장이 같은 뜻이 되도록 만드세요.

> 보기 Kim brought us some cookies. (to)
> → Kim brought some cookies to us.

1 Donna gave them her old skirts. (to)
→ _____

2 My mother cooked us some delicious spaghetti. (for)
→ _____

3 Mike does not have a bike. I will lend him it. (to)
→ Mike does not have a bike. _____

4 Dan bought his son a brand-new cell phone. (for)
→ _____

E 문장을 완성하기 위하여 가장 적절한 전치사를 쓰세요. 전치사가 필요 없으면 X 표 하세요.

1 John gave this necklace _____ me.

2 Linda made a healthy meal _____ her mother.

3 We made our children _____ model airplanes.

4 The passengers showed their tickets _____ her.

5 My aunt bought a robot _____ my little brother.

F 주어진 단어들을 바르게 배열하여 문장을 완성하세요. (참고: 영어는 항상 '주어'를 먼저 찾아야 해요.)

1 an interesting book / sent / They / me

   → _____

   (그들은 내게 흥미로운 책을 보냈다.)

2 our passports / We / them / should show

   → _____

   (우리는 그들에게 우리의 여권을 보여주어야 한다.)

3 French / Ms.Taylor / to us / teaches

   → _____

   (Taylor 선생님은 우리에게 프랑스어를 가르친다.)

4 a new watch / bought / for me / My uncle

   → _____

   (나의 삼촌은 내게 새 시계를 사주었다.)

Unit 08 수여동사

Part 3 Writing Practice

A 주어진 단어들을 활용하여 문장을 영작하세요.

album 앨범	backpack 책가방	bring 가져오다	dessert 디저트, 후식
for now 지금은	hand 도움(의 손길)	information 정보	lend 빌려주다
show 보여주다	some 약간의, 몇 개의	uncle 삼촌	useful 유용한

1 나는 Mac에게 나의 앨범을 보여주었다.

→ _____

(나는 / 보여주었다 / Mac에게 / 나의 앨범을)

2 너는 내게 도움을 주겠니? (will)

→ _____

(하겠니 / 너는 / 주다 / 내게 / 도움을)

3 나의 삼촌은 내게 책가방을 사주었다.

→ _____

(나의 삼촌은 / 사주었다 / 내게 / 책가방을)

4 Amy는 우리에게 매우 유용한 정보를 보냈다.

→ _____

(Amy는 / 보냈다 / 우리에게 / (약간의) 매우 유용한 / 정보를)

5 Tina는 우리에게 약간의 디저트를 가져왔다.

→ _____

(Tina는 / 가져왔다 / 우리에게 / 약간의 디저트를)

6 지금은 내가 너에게 10달러를 빌려줄 수 있다.

→ _____

(내가 / 할 수 있다 / 빌려주다 / 너에게 / 10달러를 / 지금은)

B 주어진 단어들을 활용하여 단락을 완성하세요.

as ~로	camera 카메라	gift 선물	often 종종	photo 사진

1 _____. Last time, I
(Tony는 / 종종 / 빌려준다 / 내게 / 몇 권의 좋은 책들을)   지난 번

borrowed a detective story from him. It was very interesting story, and I really
빌렸다   추리소설

liked it. _____.
(그는 / 주었다 / 내게 / 그 책을 / 선물로)

2 I was happy when _____. They were
(Ken은 / 보냈다 / 내게 / 몇 장의 사진들을)

the photos we took when we went on a field trip. I didn't bring my camera that
우리가 찍은 사진들   현장학습   가져오다

day. So, _____.
(그는 / 빌려주었다 / 내게 / 그의 카메라를)

C 그림을 묘사해 보세요.

My mom _____ _____ a pair of inline skates two years ago.
(나의 엄마는 2년 전에 내게 인라인 스케이트를 사주었다.)

맞다
But now they do not fit my feet.
(하지만 지금은 인라인 스케이트가 내 발에 맞지 않는다.)

사촌
So I _____ them _____ my cousin last week. (그래서 나는 지난주에 그것들을 나의 사촌에게 보냈다.)

She _____ _____ a thank-you letter today.
(그녀는 오늘 내게 고맙다는 편지를 보내왔다.)

* 주요 어휘는 Word Test p.115에서 한 번 더 연습하세요.

Unit 09 지각동사와 사역동사

Part 1 Grammar Point

A ① 지각동사는 지각, 감각을 말하는 동사입니다. 사람이나 동물이 길을 찾거나 사냥감을 찾을 때 사용하는 필수 감각들이며 생존과 밀접하게 관련이 있으므로 강조합니다.
② 목적어에 대한 보충 설명을 위해서 바로 뒤에 목적보어(O.C)를 써줍니다.

> 지각동사(see, hear, watch, feel 등) + 목적어 + 목적보어(동사원형)

- We **saw** him **enter** the building. — 우리는 그가 건물에 들어가는 것을 보았다.
- He **watched** his team **play** a game. — 그는 자신의 팀이 경기하는 것을 보았다.
- The policeman **looked** at the thief **run** away. — 경찰관은 도둑이 도망가는 것을 보았다.
- She **heard** her children **laugh** loudly. — 그녀는 자신의 아이들이 큰 소리로 웃는 것을 들었다.

* 지각동사가 있는 문장의 목적보어 자리에 현재분사(동사 + ing)가 올 수 있는데, 이때는 동작의 진행을 강조합니다.

B ① 사역동사(=노동동사)는 '~가 어떤 일을 하게 시키는' 의미의 동사입니다.
② 목적어에 대한 보충 설명을 위해서 바로 뒤에 목적보어(O.C)를 써줍니다.

> 사역동사(make, help, have, let) + 목적어 + 목적보어(동사원형)

- My daughter always **makes** me **smile**. — 내 딸은 항상 나를 미소 짓게 만든다.
- Helen **let** us **use** her phone. — Helen은 우리에게 자신의 전화를 쓰도록 해주었다.
- Mary **had** the repairman **fix** her computer. — Mary는 수리공에게 자신의 컴퓨터를 수리하게 했다.

* help는 to부정사와 동사원형을 목적격보어로 갖습니다.
  I **helped** her to move the table.
  I **helped** her move the table.

Part 2 Grammar Exercise

A 주어진 상황과 가장 알맞는 동사를 골라 문장을 완성하세요.

let	see	hear
허락하다, 놔두다	보다	듣다

1. I _____ Tommy go to school every morning.

2. We _____ him play the guitar.
   연주하다

3. _____ me introduce myself to you.
   소개하다

B 동사의 사용이 문법적으로 올바른 것을 고르세요.

1. They saw the dog (run / to run) with Tony.

2. We heard John (snore / to snore) last night.

3. Mom let me (going out / go out) and (play / to play) soccer.
   허락해주다

4. I listened to the children (talk / to talk) each other.
   들었다

5. Our teacher had us (write / to write) a 5-page report.
   시켰다

Unit 09 지각동사와 사역동사

C 단어를 바르게 배열해서 문장을 완성하세요.

> 보기 We play saw Jake the guitar.
>   (③) (①) (②)

1 Hank us had clean the windows.
     ( ) ( ) ( )

2 Tim heard yell his mother downstairs.
      ( ) ( )   ( )   아래층

3 They say let us what we think.
      ( ) ( ) ( )

4 He her had sew a button on his coat.
    ( ) ( ) ( )

D 주어진 사역동사를 사용해서 내용은 같지만, 뉘앙스는 다른 문장으로 고쳐보세요.

> 보기 Janet wanted us to come to her house. (made)
> → Janet made us come to her house.

1 Jane allowed me to see her photo album. (let)
   → Jane _____ her photo album.

2 Beth wanted her son to keep a diary. (helped)
                            일기를 쓰다
   → Beth _____ a diary.

3 We wanted the waiter to bring us some water. (had)
   → We _____ us some water.

4 My parents don't allow me to stay out late. (let)
   → My parents don't _____ late.

MUST-HAVE 3

E 동일한 내용이 되도록 사역동사를 사용해서 한 문장으로 만드세요.

> 보기 I saw them. They danced on the stage.
> → I saw them dance on the stage.

1 She made me. I bought some milk for her.
   → _____

2 They heard him. He talked on the phone.
   → _____

3 He let us. We played the board game after school.
   → _____

4 We watched her. She slept on the couch.
                              잤다
   → _____

F 주어진 단어들을 바르게 배열하여 문장을 완성하세요.(참고: 영어는 항상 '주어'를 먼저 찾아야 해요.)

1 made / fall asleep / The speech / me
            잠에 빠지다
   → _____
   (그 연설은 나를 잠들게 했다.)

2 from the sky / I saw / a star / fall down
                                    떨어지다
   → _____
   (나는 하늘에서 별이 떨어지는 것을 보았다.)

3 I helped / prepare for / Young / the interview
   → _____
   (나는 Young이 인터뷰를 준비하는 것을 도와주었다.)

4 let you / what happened / know / Ken will
   → _____
   (Ken이 너에게 무슨 일이 일어났는지 알려줄 것이다.)

Unit 09 지각동사와 사역동사

Part 3 Writing Practice

A 주어진 단어들을 활용하여 문장을 영작하세요.

breakfast 아침 식사	bully 괴롭히다	coach 코치	final 최종의	finish 끝내다
friend 친구	match 시합	never 절대 ~ 않는	practice 연습하다	report 보고서
run away 도망가다	skip 거르다	talk about ~에 대해 말하다		

1 우리 코치는 최종 시합을 위해 우리에게 연습하도록 시켰다. (have)

→ _____

(우리 코치는 / 시켰다 / 우리에게 / 연습하다 / 최종 시합을 위해)

2 너는 내가 그 보고서를 끝내는 것을 도와주겠니? (Don't로 시작하는 의문문)

→ _____

(해주겠니 / 너는 / 돕다 / 내가 / 끝내다 / 그 보고서를)

3 그들이 너를 괴롭히게 놔두지 마. (let)

→ _____

(놔두지 마 / 그들이 / 괴롭히다 / 너를)

4 나의 엄마는 내가 절대 아침을 거르지 않게 했다. (let)

→ _____

(나의 엄마는 / 절대 ~하지 않게 하다 / 내가 / 거르다 / 아침(식사)을)

5 Cindy는 그들이 그녀의 친구에 대해 말하고 있는 것을 들었다.

→ _____

(Cindy는 / 들었다 / 그들이 / ~에 대해 말하다 / 그녀의 친구)

6 Tammy는 우리가 큰 고양이로부터 도망가는 것을 보았다.

→ _____

(Tammy는 / 보았다 / 우리가 / 도망가다 / 큰 고양이로부터)

B 주어진 단어들을 활용하여 단락을 완성하세요.

| cry 울다 | living room 거실 | many 많은 | movie 영화 |
| people 사람들 | sister 여동생 | take a walk 산책하다 | weather 날씨 |

1 We went to the park with our dog. _____
(우리는 / 보았다 / 많은 사람들이 /

_____. _____
산책하고 있는 것을)   (우리는 / 들었다 / 많은 사람들이 / 이야기하는 것을 /

_____. It was a wonderful day.
날씨에 대해)

2 I saw a very sad movie at the theater last night. _____
(그 영화는 / 만들었다 / 나를 /

_____. When I came home, _____
울게)   (나는 / 들었다 / 내 여동생이 / 울고 있는 것을 /

_____. She was also watching a sad movie on TV.
거실에서)

C 그림을 묘사해 보세요.

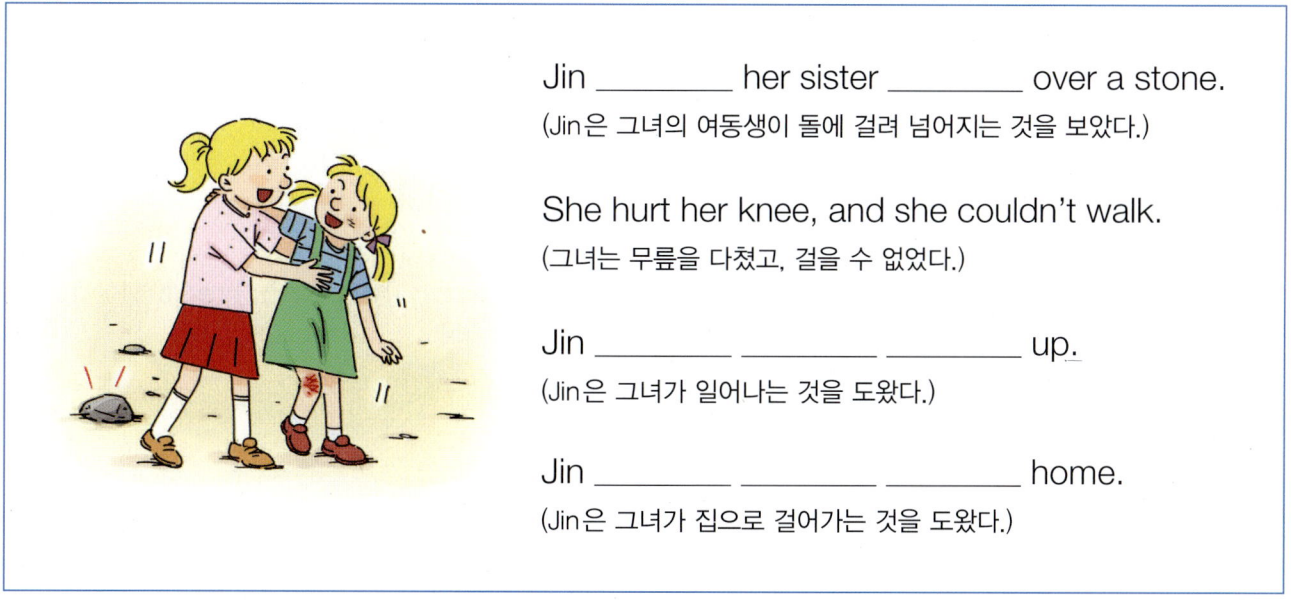

Jin _____ her sister _____ over a stone.
(Jin은 그녀의 여동생이 돌에 걸려 넘어지는 것을 보았다.)

She hurt her knee, and she couldn't walk.
(그녀는 무릎을 다쳤고, 걸을 수 없었다.)

Jin _____ _____ _____ up.
(Jin은 그녀가 일어나는 것을 도왔다.)

Jin _____ _____ _____ home.
(Jin은 그녀가 집으로 걸어가는 것을 도왔다.)

* 주요 어휘는 Word Test p.116에서 한 번 더 연습하세요.

Review 03: Narrative Essay

A 아래 표를 참고하여, 가장 행복했던 순간에 대한 글에 들어갈 내용을 정리하세요.

When did it happen? 언제	as soon as I came home from school
Where did it happen? 어디서	in my room
What happened? 무엇이	My dad gave me the piano.
How did you feel? 어떻게	very excited 흥분된/신난
What happened after? 후에	My family saw me play the piano. I made them smile.

OUTLINE

Title The Happiest Moment in My Life
    가장 행복한   순간

Beginning when I got a surprise present from my dad
    얻었다/받았다   선물

Middle
- _____ _____ _____ I came home from school, I saw a new piano.
- My dad _____ _____ _____ _____.
- I was very excited.
- Even though I was not good at playing the piano, I really liked it.
- My family _____ _____ _____ the piano.

Ending I _____ _____ _____.

MUST-HAVE 3

B 아웃라인을 바탕으로 행복했던 순간에 대한 에세이를 완성하세요.

The Happiest Moment in My Life — Title

The happiest moment in my life was _____
_____ from my dad.
— Beginning

I remember that day very clearly. _____ I came home from school, I _____ in my room. My dad _____ as a surprise present. I _____ because of the new piano. I couldn't wait to play it. _____
_____, I really liked it. My family _____ every day.
— Middle

Whenever I played the piano, I _____.
~할 때는 언제나
— Ending

아래 내용을 모두 잘 학습하였으면 □안에 ✓하세요.

☐ 부사절을 만드는 접속사를 맞게 사용하였다.

☐ 수여동사를 맞게 사용하였다.

☐ 지각동사와 사역동사를 맞게 사용하였다.

Unit 10 현재완료

Part 1 Grammar Point

A 현재완료는 [have + 과거분사 (p.p.)]의 형태로 과거에 일어난 일이 현재까지 영향을 미치는 것을 말합니다. 주어가 3인칭 단수인 경우 [has + p.p]가 됩니다.

- I **have** just **eaten** a hamburger. 나는 방금 햄버거를 먹었다. (지금은 햄버거가 없다는 의미)
- I **have known** him for 12 years. 나는 그를 안지 12년이 되었다. (12년 전부터 알고, 지금도 그를 안다는 의미)
- She **has turned** on the laptop. 그녀는 노트북 컴퓨터를 켜 놓았다. (지금도 켜있다는 의미)

B 현재완료의 부정문은 have/has 뒤에 not을 쓰고, 의문문은 Have/Has를 주어 앞에 씁니다.

형태	부정문	의문문
have/has + p.p.	have/has + not + p.p.	Have/Has + 주어 + p.p.~?

* have not은 haven't로 has not은 hasn't로 줄여 쓸 수 있어요.

- I **haven't learned** Japanese before. 나는 전에 일본어를 배운 적이 없다.
- She **hasn't done** her homework yet. 그녀는 아직 숙제를 하지 않았다.
- A: **Have** you **been** to Canada? 캐나다에 가본 적 있니?
  B: Yes, I **have**. / No, I **haven't**. 응, 가본 적 있어. / 아니, 가본 적 없어.

* 불규칙 변화 동사표는 Appendix p.108-109 참고

C 확실한 과거를 나타내는 단어는 현재완료와 함께 사용하지 마세요.

- I have seen Julie yesterday. (X) → I **saw** Julie yesterday. 나는 어제 Julie를 보았다.
- I've gone to America in 2020. (X) → I **went** to America in 2020. 나는 2020년도에 미국에 갔다.

* 확실한 과거를 나타내는 말은 yesterday, ago, last, in 2021 (해, 년) 등입니다.

MUST-HAVE 3

Part 2 Grammar Exercise

A 현재완료 시제를 사용해서 주어진 상황을 설명하세요.

drive	play	lose
운전하다	놀다, 경기하다	잃어버리다

1 We _____ basketball for more than two hours.

2 Ms. Smith _____ a car since 2020.
~이후로

3 Ian _____ his umbrella recently.
최근에

B 인칭과 시제가 모두 맞도록 현재완료형 문장을 완성하세요.

1 She (have / has) _____ her purse in the mall. (lose)
지갑(여성용)

2 We (have / has) _____ in China for five months now. (stay)

3 Kelly (have / has) _____ interested in playing chess since last year. (be)

4 It (have / has) _____ since last week. (rain)

5 I (have / has) _____ as a mechanic since I graduated from school. (work)
정비사   졸업했다

69

Unit 10 현재완료

C 현재완료형이 사용된 문장을 부정문, 의문문으로 바꾸세요.

1. Paula has eaten lunch at the restaurant. (부정문)
   → _____

2. Brian has bought a brand-new suit. (의문문)
   → _____

3. Linda has seen her brother for two months. (부정문)
   → _____

4. She has talked about the concert with him. (의문문)
   → _____

5. Ted has locked his keys in his car. (부정문)
      잠가 두었다/고정시켰다
   → _____

D 시제가 정확해지도록 밑줄 친 부분을 고쳐 쓰세요.

1. It has snowed last night.
   → It _____ last night.

2. I took his class since last week.
   → I _____ his class since last week.

3. She has gone to the city museum last month.
   → She _____ to the city museum last month.

4. I knew Mary since I was ten.
   → I _____ Mary since I was ten.

E 내용상 가장 정확한 시제를 고르세요.

1. I bought a puppy two years ago. I still have the puppy.
   → I (had / **have had**) the puppy for two years.

2. She started her vacation last Saturday. She is still on vacation now.
   → She (was / **has been**) on vacation since last Saturday.

3. We met each other ten years ago. We still know each other.
   → We (knew / **have known**) each other for ten years now.

4. Emily lived in New York three years ago, but she is not in New York anymore.
   → Emily (**lived** / has lived) in New York three years ago.

F 주어진 단어들을 바르게 배열하여 문장을 완성하세요.(참고: 영어는 항상 '주어'를 먼저 찾아야 해요.)

1. have taken / for two years / I / tennis lessons
   → _____
   (나는 2년 동안 테니스 레슨을 받아왔다.)

2. Have / to another country / ever been / you
   → _____
   (너는 다른 나라에 가본 적이 있니?)

3. our plan / We / three times / have checked
   → _____
   (우리는 우리의 계획을 세 번 점검했다.)

4. never heard / They / such an interesting story / have
   → _____
   (그들은 그렇게 흥미로운 이야기를 들어본 적이 없었다.)

Unit 10 현재완료

Part 3 Writing Practice

A 주어진 단어들을 활용하여 문장을 영작하세요.

email 이메일	get 받다	just 방금	lose 잃어버리다
math 수학	old 오래된	German freind 독일 친구	perfect score 만점
preschool 유치원	since 이후로	study 공부하다	test 시험

1 우리는 이 오래된 TV를 2015년 이후로 가지고 있다.

→ _____

(우리는 / 가지고 있다 / 이 오래된 TV를 / 2015년 이후로)

2 Nick은 그의 자동차 열쇠를 잃어버렸다. 지금도 가지고 있지 않다.

→ _____ He doesn't have it now.

(Nick은 / 잃어버렸다 / 그의 자동차 열쇠를)

3 나는 방금 내 독일 친구로부터 이메일을 받았다.

→ _____

(나는 / 방금 / 받았다 / 이메일을 / 내 독일 친구로부터)

4 그들은 유치원 때부터 친구였다.

→ _____

(그들은 / 였다 / 친구 / 유치원 때부터)

5 나는 3년 동안 수학을 공부를 해왔다.

→ _____

(나는 / 공부를 해왔다 / 수학을 / 3년 동안)

6 너는 시험에서 만점을 받은 적 있니?

→ _____

(너는 / 받은 적 있니 / 만점을 / 시험에서)

MUST-HAVE 3

B 주어진 단어들을 활용하여 단락을 완성하세요.

| all 모든 | a lot of 많은 | be born 태어나다 | enjoy 즐기다 | hometown 고향 |
| leave 떠나다 | live 살다 | outdoor activity 야외활동 | sunshine 햇빛 | |

1. _____ . _____
   (Sam은 / 떠난 적이 없었다 / 그의 고향을)   (그는 / 살아왔다 /

   _____ . Still, he is happy
   그의 고향에서 / 이후로 / 그가 태어난)

   with his friends and family.

2. It has been sunny all week. _____
   화창하다/날씨가 맑다   (우리는 / 했다 / 많은 / 야외 활동들을)

   for this week. _____ . I hope to
                  (우리는 / 즐겼다 / 모든 / 햇빛을)

   have this nice weather next week, too.

C 그림을 묘사해 보세요.

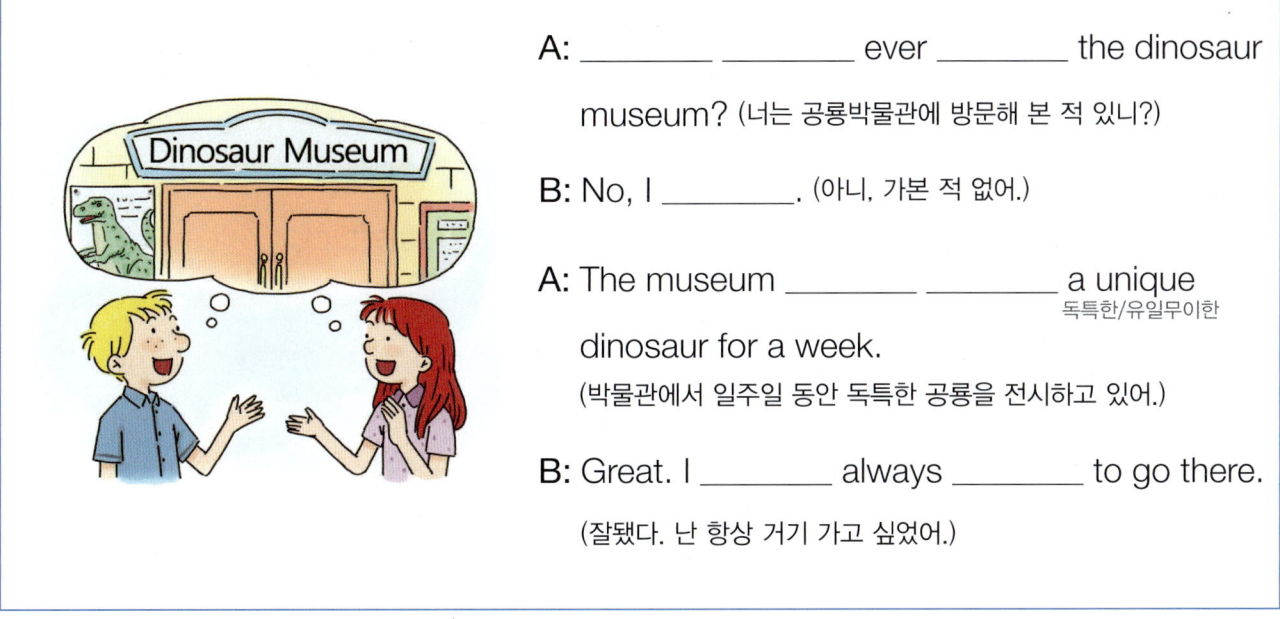

A: _____ _____ ever _____ the dinosaur museum? (너는 공룡박물관에 방문해 본 적 있니?)

B: No, I _____. (아니, 가본 적 없어.)

A: The museum _____ _____ a unique dinosaur for a week.
독특한/유일무이한
(박물관에서 일주일 동안 독특한 공룡을 전시하고 있어.)

B: Great. I _____ always _____ to go there.
(잘됐다. 난 항상 거기 가고 싶었어.)

* 주요 어휘는 Word Test p.116에서 한 번 더 연습하세요.

Unit 11 비교급

Part 1 Grammar Point

A ① 비교급은 두 대상을 비교할 때 '~보다 더 …한/하게'라는 의미입니다.
② [비교급 + than]이 기본적인 형태입니다.

> **원급** He is old. 그는 나이가 들었다.   **비교급** He is **older than** me. 그는 나보다 나이가 더 들었다.

B 비교급은 형용사나 부사에 '-er'을 붙인 형태가 일반적입니다. 하지만 음절과 단어 길이에 따라서 약간의 예외가 있어요.

형용사/부사	규 칙	예 시
1음절, 일부 2음절	-er	kind → kind**er**, fast → fast**er**
자음 + y	-y → -i + -er	happy → happ**ier**, early → earl**ier**
단모음 + 단자음	끝자음 + -er	hot → hot**ter**, big → big**ger**
대부분의 2, 3음절 이상	**more** + 형용사/부사	beautiful → **more** beautiful, famous → **more** famous
불규칙 변화	good / well → **better**, bad / badly → **worse**, many / much → **more**, little → **less**, late → **later** / **latter**	

- You look **thinner than** before.   너는 지난번보다 더 말라 보인다.
- Health is **more** important **than** money.   건강이 돈보다 더 중요하다.

C [as + 형용사/부사 + as]는 '~만큼 …한/하게'라는 의미입니다.

- My sister is **as tall as** I am.   내 여동생은 나만큼 키가 크다.
- This summer is **as hot as** last summer.   이번 여름은 지난 여름만큼 덥다.

D [the + 비교급, the + 비교급]은 '~할수록, 더 …하다'라는 의미입니다.

- **The more, the better.**   많을수록 더 좋다.
- **The higher** we climb, **the colder** the air becomes.   우리가 높이 올라갈수록, 공기는 더 차가워진다.

E [get + 비교급 (+ and 비교급)]은 '점점 더 ~해지다'라는 의미입니다.

- His illness is **getting better**.   그의 병세는 점점 좋아지고 있다.
- It's **getting colder and colder**.   날씨가 점점 더 추워진다.

Part 2 Grammar Exercise

A 다음 형용사와 부사의 비교급을 쓰세요.

1. thin → _____ (더 얇은)
   얇은
2. strong → _____ ( )
   강한
3. healthy → _____ ( )
   건강한
4. handsome → _____ (더 잘생긴)
   잘생긴
5. famous → _____ ( )
   유명한
6. much → _____ ( )
   많은
7. late → _____ ( )
   늦은
8. interesting → _____ ( )
   흥미있는

B 형용사를 비교급으로 바꿔서 주어진 상황을 설명하세요.

> fast → _____ , big → _____ , difficult → _____
> 빠른   큰   어려운, 힘든

1.  My hands are _____ than yours.

2.  The plane is _____ than the train.

3. Math is _____ than English for me.

Unit 11 비교급

C 밑줄 친 부분이 올바른 비교급 모습이 되도록 고치세요.

1 This melon is as <u>bigger</u> as that one.
  → This melon is as _____ as that one.

2 My accent is <u>bad</u> than yours.
  억양
  → My accent is _____ than yours.

3 Gary is <u>heavyer</u> than Mike.
  → Gary is _____ than Mike.

4 The tree is growing <u>tall and tall</u>.
  자라는
  → The tree is growing _____.

D 비교급을 사용해서 두 문장을 한 문장으로 완성하세요.

> 보기 Eric is 16 years old. Mike is 14 years old.
> → <u>Eric is older than Mike.</u> (old)

1 My desk is 2.5 meters long. Yours is 2 meters long.
  긴
  → _____ (long)

2 I am 160cm tall. My younger sister is 155cm tall.
  키가 큰
  → _____ (tall)

3 This year, the temperature is 33°C in summer. Last year, it was 30°C in summer.
  금년   온도   작년
  → _____ (hot)

4 A laptop is 900,000 won. A cell phone is 1,000,000 won.
  → _____ (expensive)

E 주어진 질문에 대해서 비교급이 사용된 문장으로 대답하세요.

> 보기 Q: Which is bigger, pineapples or apples? (pineapples)
> A: <u>Pineapples are bigger than apples.</u>

1 Q: Which is smaller, this city or that city? (this city)
   A: _____

2 Q: Which is cheaper, this camera or that camera? (that camera)
   A: _____

3 Q: Who swims faster, Jim or Alex? (Alex)
   A: _____

4 Q: Which is more difficult, math or science? (science)
   A: _____

F 주어진 단어들을 바르게 배열하여 문장을 완성하세요.(참고: 영어는 항상 '주어'를 먼저 찾아야 해요.)

1 my mother / is older / My father / than

   → _____
   (나의 아버지는 나의 어머니보다 연세가 많다.)

2 Chinese / is not / English / as easy as

   → _____
   (중국어는 영어만큼 쉽지 않다.)

3 is getting / Science / more advanced

   → _____
   (과학이 점점 더 발전하고 있다.)

4 more slowly / than / My computer works / my friend's

   → _____
   (내 컴퓨터가 내 친구의 것보다 더 느리게 작동한다.)

Unit 11 비교급

Part 3 Writing Practice

A 주어진 단어들을 활용하여 문장을 영작하세요.

about ~에 대해	bright 밝은	brother 남자 형제	busy 붐비는
creative 창의적인	dress 드레스	fancy 화려한	history 역사
know 알다	long 긴	moon 달	street 거리

1 태양은 달보다 더 밝다.

→ _____

(태양은 / 더 밝다 / 달보다)

2 그녀는 나보다 역사에 대해 더 많이 안다.

→ _____

(그녀는 / 안다 / 더 많이 / 역사에 대해 / 나보다)

3 Kevin은 그의 형만큼 창의적이다.

→ _____

(Kevin은 / 이다 / ~만큼 / 창의적인 / 그의 형)

4 낮이 점점 더 길어지고 있다.

→ _____

(낮이 / ~해지다 / 점점 더 길어지는)

5 그 빨간 드레스가 노란 드레스보다 더 화려하다.

→ _____

(그 빨간 드레스가 / 더 화려하다 / 그 노란 드레스보다)

6 그 거리는 점점 더 붐비고 있었다.

→ _____

(그 거리는 / ~해지고 있었다 / 점점 더 붐비는)

MUST-HAVE 3

B 주어진 단어들을 활용하여 단락을 완성하세요.

beautiful 아름다운	comic book 만화책	interesting 재미있는
like 좋아한다	novel 소설	read 읽다
singer 가수	sister 여자 형제	voice 목소리

1 My favorite singer is Sandra. _____
   가장 좋아하는   (그녀의 목소리는 / 이다 / 더 아름다운 / ~보다)

other singers'. _____.
              (나의 여동생은 / 좋아한다 / 그녀를 / ~만큼 / 내가 (좋아)하는)

We will go to her concert someday.
                          언젠가

2 My parents want me to read novels. But I like comic books very much. _____
                           소설책들   만화책들

_____. _____
(만화책은 / 이다 / 더 재미있는 / ~보다 / 소설)   (~할수록 / 내가 읽다 /

_____.
       더 / 나는 즐긴다)

C 그림을 묘사해 보세요.

At first, I _____ _____ _____ my brother in every way.
(처음에 나는 모든 면에서 내 동생보다 나았다.)

However, he is _____ _____ _____

_____. (그러나 그는 점점 더 똑똑해지고 있다.)

Now, he _____ _____ _____ than I do.
(지금은 그가 나보다 더 나은 점수를 받는다.)

* 주요 어휘는 Word Test p.117에서 한 번 더 연습하세요.

Unit 12 수와 양을 나타내기

Grammar Point

A 수와 양을 말할 때 매우 많이 사용되는 9개의 표현이 있습니다.
매일 사용하는 표현이므로 외워두세요.

구 분	형 태		의 미
수	a couple of	+ 셀 수 있는 명사의 복수	2~3개의
	a few		몇 개의
	several		여러 개의
	many		많은 (= a number of)
양	a little	+ 셀 수 없는 명사의 단수	약간의, 조금의
	much		많은
수, 양 모두	some	+ 셀 수 있는 명사의 복수 셀 수 없는 명사의 단수	몇몇, 조금의
	a lot of		많은 (= lots of, plenty of)
	most		대부분의

수

- There are **a couple of** examples of this theory.   이 이론의 2~3가지 예가 있다.
- I need **a few** hours to finish this work.   이 작업을 끝내려면 몇 시간이 필요하다.
- We took **several** pictures at the picnic.   우리는 소풍에서 여러 장의 사진을 찍었다.
- We have **a number of** events before the end of the term.   우리는 학기말 전에 많은 행사가 있다.

양

- I put **a little** salt in the soup.   나는 수프에 약간의 소금을 넣었다.
- She doesn't have **much** money.   그녀는 많은 돈을 가지고 있지 않다.

수와 양

- We planted **some** flowers in the garden.   우리는 정원에 약간의 꽃을 심었다.
- Orange juices have **a lot of** vitamin C.   오렌지 주스에는 많은 비타민C가 있다.
- **Most** people at the airport looked excited.   공항에 있는 대부분의 사람들은 들떠 보였다.

Part 2 Grammar Exercise

A 적절한 수와 양을 선택해서 주어진 상황을 설명해 보세요.

a little	a few	many
약간의, 조금 (셀 수 없음)	약간의, 조금 (셀 수 있음)	많음 (셀 수 있음)

1 Roy gave me _____ candies in a basket.

2 I have _____ money now.

3 There are _____ balloons in the sky.
~이 있다

B 문장 속에 사용된 명사의 수와 양을 가장 알맞게 표현한 것을 고르세요.

1 I have (a little / a lot of) reasons to go there.

2 I want to recommend (much / several) books.
추천하다

3 We had (a few / a little) rain this morning.

4 They invited (a number of / much) guests to the party.
손님들

5 He doesn't have (many / much) information.
정보

Unit 12 수와 양을 나타내기

C many / much 또는 a few / a little을 넣어 문장을 완성하세요. (중복사용 가능)

1 I'm late. I don't have _____ time now.

2 I love tomatoes, so I bought _____ tomatoes.

3 I need _____ close friends. I don't need many.
　　　　　　　　　　　　가까운/친한

4 Mac doesn't drink _____ water. He usually drinks soda.
　　　　　　　　　　　　　　　　　　　　　　　보통/대개

5 I don't know much about music. I only know _____.

D 수와 양을 표현하는 단어를 사용하여 주어진 문장을 완성하세요.

> 보기 Sam didn't have any friends at first. (several)
> → But now Sam has several friends.

1 I had five cards, but I gave him three of them. (a couple of)

→ Now, I have _____.

2 Tony couldn't buy much sugar. (a little)

→ So he bought _____.

3 I want to make omelets for two. There is only one egg left. (some)
　　　　　　　　　　　　　　　　　　　　　　　　　　　　　　남은

→ So I need to buy _____.

4 We wanted take many pictures, and we had enough time. (a lot of)
　　　　　　　　　　　　찍다

→ So we took _____.

E 다음 밑줄 친 부분이 틀린 부분이 있으면 고치고, 없으면 X표 하세요.

1 We had a lot of rain last year. (   )

2 I gave him many money. (   )

3 There is a few soda left in the fridge. (   )

4 The baby drinks plenty of milk every day. (   )
   　　　　　　　　　충분한

5 Jenny has much friends in her class. (   )

F 주어진 단어들을 바르게 배열하여 문장을 완성하세요. (참고: 영어는 항상 '주어*'를 먼저 찾아야 해요.)

1 a number of / in the library / There were* / students

   → _____
   (도서관에는 많은 학생들이 있었다.)

2 to grow / sunshine / Plants need* / a lot of

   → _____
   (식물이 자라기 위해서는 많은 햇빛이 필요하다.)

3 to go on a trip / a few / days off / My father took*

   → _____
   (나의 아버지는 여행을 가기 위해 며칠 휴가를 냈다.)

4 in the earthquake / Most of the buildings* / were destroyed
   　　　　　　　　　　　　　　　　　　　　　　　　　　　파괴된

   → _____
   (건물 대부분이 지진으로 파괴되었다.)

Unit 12 수와 양을 나타내기

Part 3 Writing Practice

A 주어진 단어들을 활용하여 문장을 영작하세요.

> drink 마시다
> in the river 강에
> make a friend 친구를 사귀다
> write 쓰다
> fly around ~의 주위를 날다
> in the universe 우주에
> mosquito 모기
> in the future 미래에
> letter 편지
> wine 포도주

1 Ben은 그녀에게 두 세 통의 편지를 썼다. (a couple of)

→ _____

(Ben은 / 썼다* / 그녀에게 / 두 세 통의 편지를)

2 우주에는 수많은 별들이 있다. (a large number of) (There are ~)

→ _____

(있다 / 수많은 별들이* / 우주에는)

3 나의 아빠는 포도주를 많이 마시지 않는다.

→ _____

(나의 아빠는 / 마시지 않는다* / 많은 포도주를)

4 강에는 많은 물고기들이 있지 않다. (many) (There are not ~)

→ _____

(있지 않다 / 많은 물고기들이* / 강에는)

5 나는 미래에 많은 친구들을 사귀고 싶다. (a lot of)

→ _____

(나는* / 하고 싶다 / 사귀다 / 많은 친구들을 / 미래에)

6 나는 몇 마리의 모기들이 내 주위를 날아다니는 것을 보았다. (a few)

→ _____

(나는* / 보았다 / 몇 마리의 모기들이 / 내 주위를 날아다니는 것을)

B 주어진 단어들을 활용하여 단락을 완성하세요.

| green 녹색의 | leaf 잎 | money 돈 | new 새로운 |
| now 지금 | problem 문제 | yard 마당 | |

1 Today is my sister's birthday. I want to buy her a great gift. But _____
(나는 /

_____. _____
가지고 있다 / 몇 개의 / 문제를)   (나는 / 가지고 있지 않다 / 많은 /

_____. I need to think of some other choices.
돈을 / 지금은)   다른   선택들/선택권들

2 James has a big yard at his house. There are _____
           마당   (여러 개의 나무들이 / 마당에)

In spring, _____.
           (그 나무들은 / 가진다 / 많은 / 초록색 잎들을)

When we have plenty of rain, they look greener.
              많은   더 녹색/더 파란

C 그림을 묘사해 보세요.

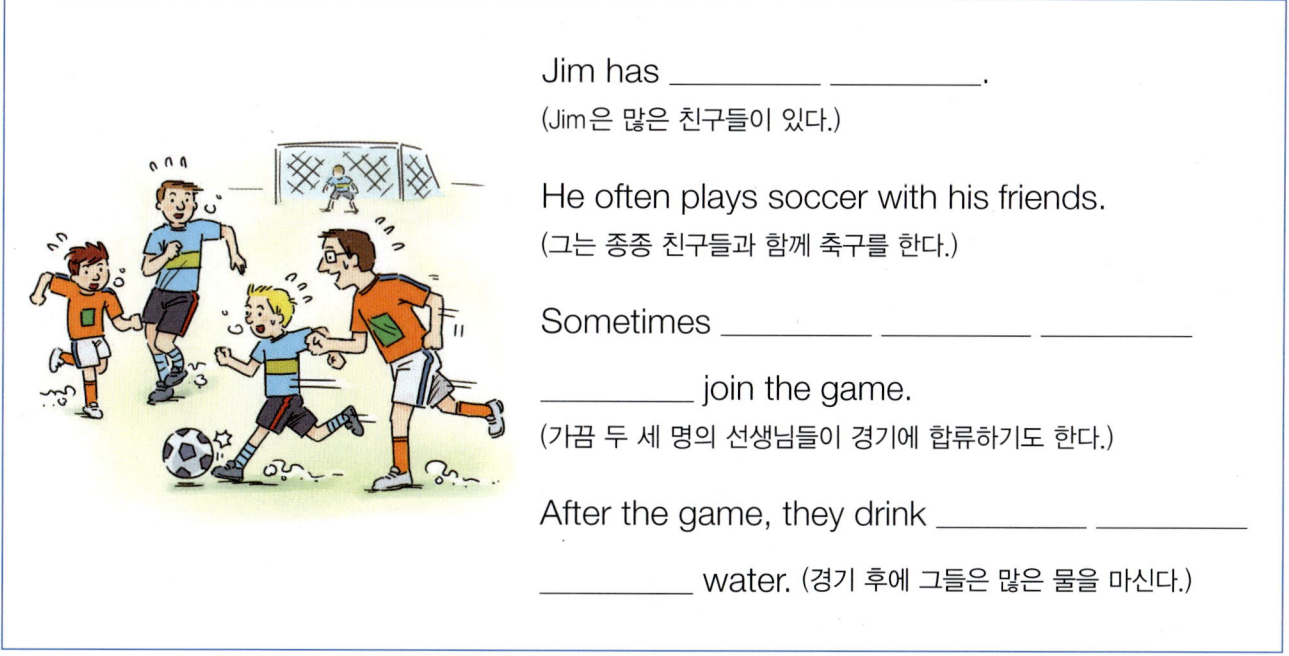

Jim has _____ _____.
(Jim은 많은 친구들이 있다.)

He often plays soccer with his friends.
(그는 종종 친구들과 함께 축구를 한다.)

Sometimes _____ _____ _____

_____ join the game.
(가끔 두 세 명의 선생님들이 경기에 합류하기도 한다.)

After the game, they drink _____ _____

_____ water. (경기 후에 그들은 많은 물을 마신다.)

＊ 주요 어휘는 Word Test p.117에서 한 번 더 연습하세요.

Review 04 Report

A 아래 표를 참고하여, 환경 보호를 위한 방법을 제시하는 글에 들어갈 내용을 정리하세요.

Suggestions 제안(들)	Purposes 목적(들)
use a cup when brushing teeth	help not waste a lot of water (낭비하다)
ride my bike to school	more efficient way to reduce air pollution (효과적인 / 줄이다)
unplug the electronics (뽑다)	save both electricity and money (둘 다 / 전기)

OUTLINE

Title   How to Protect the Environment (보호하다/지키다)

Introduction   would like to suggest some ways and describe what I have (설명하다) done these days (했던)

Body
- have used a cup when I brush my teeth
  → help not waste _____ _____ _____ water
- have _____ my bike to school
  → is a _____ _____ way to reduce air pollution
- _____ unplugged the electronics
  → can save both electricity and money

Conclusion   Small changes can have big effects. (변화들 / 효과들)

---

air pollution 공기 오염   efficient 효율적인   electricity 전기   electronics 전자제품
environment 환경   reduce 줄이다   suggest 제안하다   unplug 플러그를 뽑다

MUST-HAVE 3

B 아웃라인을 바탕으로 환경 보호를 위한 방법을 제시하는 글을 완성하세요.

How to Protect the Environment — Title

Protecting the environment is important. I would like to
보호하는 것/지키는 것   환경   ~하기를 원하다

suggest some ways and describe _____ for the
제안하다

environment these days.

— Introduction

I _____ when I brush my teeth. It helps

not _____. I also _____

to school instead of riding in my father's car. It is _____
                                      타는 것

_____ to reduce air pollution. In addition, _____
                                게다가

_____ not in use. It can save both electricity and money.

— Body

I think these ways are easy to practice in real life. Small
                                            실제 생활
changes can have big effects.

— Conclusion

아래 내용을 모두 잘 학습하였으면 □안에 ✔하세요.

☐ 과거에서 현재까지 일어난 일을 표현하기 위해 현재완료(have/has+과거분사)를 사용하였다.

☐ 비교급을 사용하여 '~보다 …한/하게'를 맞게 표현하였다.

☐ do의 과거분사 done을 사용하였다.

Unit 13 명사절

Part 1 Grammar Point

A ① 명사절과 명사는 같은 개념입니다. 문장 속에서 주어, 목적어, 보어로 쓸 수 있어요.
② 명사절은 [that+주어+동사]의 형태로 만들면 됩니다.

- **That I like her** is true. 내가 그녀를 좋아한다는 것은 사실이다. (주어)
- Everybody knows (**that**) **I like her**. 모두가 내가 그녀를 좋아한다는 것을 안다. (목적어)
- The truth is **that I like her**. 진실은 내가 그녀를 좋아한다는 것이다. (보어)

B 명사절을 주어로 쓰면 긴 주어가 만들어져요.
주어가 길어지는 것을 피하고 싶을 때는 가주어 It으로 대체할 수 있습니다.

- That she is a genius is not true. 그녀가 천재라는 것은 사실이 아니다.
  = **It** is not true that she is a genius. (It: 가짜 주어, that she is a genius: 진짜 주어)
- That he won the game is surprising. 그가 경기에서 우승했다는 것은 놀랍다.
  = **It** is surprising that he won the game. (It: 가짜 주어, that he won the game: 진짜 주어)

C 동사(타동사) 뒤에 명사절을 목적어로 쓰면, 좀 더 길고 내용이 자세한 문장을 만들 수 있어요.

> **think**, **know**, **hear**, **remember**, **understand**, **believe**, **realize** 등 + that절 (목적어)

- I **believe** (that) Andy did his best. 나는 Andy가 최선을 다했다고 믿는다.
  (believe의 목적어)
- I **heard** (that) Hank would come back soon. 나는 Hank가 곧 돌아온다고 들었다.
  (heard의 목적어)
- We **understand** (that) you need more time. 우리는 네가 시간이 더 필요하다는 것을 이해한다.
  (understand의 목적어)

*that절이 목적어로 쓰일 때 접속사 that을 생략하는 경우가 많습니다.

D 명사절을 be동사 뒤에 보어로 쓸 수 있습니다.

- The problem is that I do not have enough time. 문제는 말이야.
  내가 충분한 시간을 가지고 있지 않다는 거지.

Part 2 Grammar Exercise

A ① 내용상 가장 적절한 동사를 고르세요.

hear	think	know
듣다	생각하다	알다

② 명사절(that+주어+동사~)을 사용해서 주어진 상황을 설명하세요.

1. I didn't _____ _____ Jen studied Chinese.

2. He _____ _____ computer games are bad for children.

3. A few days ago, they _____ _____ Mary wants to be a scientist.
   며 칠 전

B 다음 밑줄 친 명사절이 하는 역할을 주어, 보어, 목적어 중 골라 쓰세요.

1. I know that someone should do the job. _____

2. It is not true that Jane cheated on the exam. _____

3. The problem is that the police don't have any evidence. _____
   증거

4. Isn't it amazing that Sandra won a gold medal? _____
   놀라운

5. She believes that everyone supports her plan. _____
   지지하다

Unit 13 명사절

C 명사절 부분을 살려서 전체 해석을 완성하세요.

1 It is true that she came from France.
   → _____ 사실이다.

2 It is difficult for us that we master a second language.
   완전히 익히다
   → _____ 어렵다.

3 It is amazing that we have another chance.
   → _____ 놀랍다.

4 It is important that we don't break our rules.
   → _____ 중요하다.

D 보기와 같이 가주어(it)를 사용하여 문장을 바꿔 쓰세요.

> 보기 That Kim told a lie to me is clear.
> → It is clear that Kim told a lie to me.

1 That I meet my teacher is necessary.
   필요한
   → _____

2 That Ralph is married is true.
   → _____

3 That we used to call him a genius is unbelievable.
   천재   믿을 수 없는
   → _____

4 That the Earth is round is common knowledge.
   일반적인   상식/지식
   → _____

E 명사절 that(=접속사 that)을 사용해서 두 문장을 하나로 연결하세요.

> 보기 The girl broke the vase. I believe it.
> → I believe that the girl broke the vase.

1 I like her. She knows it.
→ _____

2 I made a mistake. I thought so.
→ _____

3 He passed the driving test. I don't believe it.
→ _____

4 Our team won the game. I heard it.
→ _____

F 주어진 단어들을 바르게 배열하여 문장을 완성하세요.(참고: 영어는 항상 '주어'를 먼저 찾아야 해요.)

1 Greg / Did you hear / that / became a doctor
→ _____
(너는 Greg가 의사가 된 것을 들었니?)

2 a healing effect / I believe / music has / that
→ _____
(나는 음악이 치유효과가 있다는 것을 믿는다.)

3 I think / made a big mistake / that / you
→ _____
(나는 네가 큰 실수를 했다고 생각한다.)

4 she used to / I remember / be an artist / that
→ _____
(나는 그녀가 예술가였던 것을 기억한다.)

Unit 13 명사절

Part 3 Writing Practice

A 주어진 단어들을 활용하여 문장을 영작하세요.

class president 반장	do one's best 최선을 다하다	help 돕다	important 중요한
point 점	take a bus 버스를 타다	the other day 지난번에	true 사실의
used 중고의	wrong 잘못된, 틀린		

1 우리는 Jessie가 중고 자동차를 샀다고 들었다.

→ _____

(우리는 / 들었다 / ~것을 / Jessie가 / 샀다 / 중고 자동차를)

2 중요한 점은 네가 최선을 다했다는 것이다.

→ _____

(중요한 점은 / 이다 / ~것이 / 네가 / 최선을 다했다)

3 그는 우리가 지난번에 그를 도와줬다는 것을 기억한다.

→ _____

(그는 / 기억한다 / ~것을 / 우리가 / 도와줬다 / 그를 / 지난번에)

4 Sandy가 반장이라는 것은 사실이 아니다.

→ _____

((그것은) 아니다 / 사실이 / ~것은 / Sandy가 / 반장이라는)

5 나는 Frank가 틀린 버스를 탔다는 것을 들었다.

→ _____

(나는 / 들었다 / ~것을 / Frank가 / 탔다 / 틀린 버스를)

6 네가 내 친구라는 것은 변하지 않을 것이다.

→ _____

((그것은) ~하지 않을 것이다 / 변하다 / ~것은 / 네가 / 이다 / 내 친구)

MUST-HAVE 3

B 주어진 단어들을 활용하여 단락을 완성하세요.

> great 훌륭한　　innocent 결백한　　pianist 피아니스트　　play the piano 피아노를 치다
> steal 훔치다　　very well 매우 잘　　wallet (남성용) 지갑

1 I heard that Jamie is good at playing the piano. One day, I asked him to play.
　　　　　　　　　　　　　　　　~에 능숙하다　　　　　　　　　　　　　　　어느 날

_____. _____
((그것은) 사실이었다 / ~것은 / 그가 / 피아노를 친다 / 매우 잘)　　　　　　　　(나는 /

_____.
생각한다 / ~것을 / 그가 / 될 것이다 / 훌륭한 피아니스트가)

2 The rumor is that Tom stole my wallet. _____
　　　소문, 유언비어　　　　　　훔쳤다　　　　　　　　　((그것은) 사실이 아니다 / ~것은 / 그가 /

_____. _____
훔쳤다 / 나의 지갑을)　　　　　　　(나는 / 안다 / ~것을 / Tom이 / 결백한)

He's never disappointed me.
　　　　　　실망시켰다

C 그림을 묘사해 보세요.

At first, I didn't _____ _____ I had made a mistake. (처음에 나는 내가 실수를 저질렀다는 것을 몰랐다.)

_____ _____ _____ it was someone else's fault. (나는 그것이 다른 누군가의 잘못이라고 생각했다.)
　　　　　　　　　　잘못

_____ _____ _____ I was not responsible for it. (나는 내가 그것에 책임이 없다고 믿었다.)
　　　　　　　　　　　　책임이 있는

But soon _____ _____ _____ I have done something wrong.
(그러나 곧 나는 내가 뭔가 잘못했다는 것을 깨달았다.)

＊ 주요 어휘는 Word Test p.118에서 한 번 더 연습하세요.

Unit 14 형용사절

Part 1 Grammar Point

A 형용사절은 바로 앞에 있는 명사를 수식합니다. 이 수식 받는 명사를 선행사라고 해요.

- She has a car. The car has four seats.
  → She has a car which has four seats.   그녀는 좌석이 4개 있는 자동차를 가지고 있다.
  (선행사)   (형용사절)

B 관계대명사는 주어를 대신해서 쓰는 주격, 목적어를 대신해서 쓰는 목적격, 소유를 대신해서 쓰는 소유격으로 나눠집니다. 선행사가 사람 또는 사물인지에 따라 who, which, that 중 골라 쓰면 됩니다.

종류	선행사		
	사람	동물, 사물	사람, 동물, 사물
주격 관계대명사	who	which	that
목적격 관계대명사	whom		
소유격 관계대명사	whose	whose (of which)	-

- Sally is a student. She has long hair.
  → Sally is a student **who** has long hair.   Sally는 긴 머리를 가진 학생이다. (주격)

- I like spaghetti. This has lots of cheese.
  → I like spaghetti **which** has lots of cheese.   나는 치즈가 많이 들어있는 스파게티를 좋아한다. (주격)

- These are the people. I invited them.
  → These are the people **who(m)** I invited.   이들이 내가 초대한 사람들이다. (목적격)

- Purple is the color. I like it.
  → Purple is the color **which** I like.   보라색은 내가 좋아하는 색이다. (목적격)

- I found the book. Its cover is red.
  → I found the book **whose** cover is red.   나는 표지가 빨간 책을 찾았다. (소유격)
  → I found the book **of which** the cover is red.

*that은 수식하는 명사(선행사)에 상관없이 모두 쓸 수 있으며 whom은 who로 대신 쓸 수 있어요.

Part 2 Grammar Exercise

A 적절한 관계대명사를 골라 주어진 상황을 설명하세요.

| who(m) | which | whose |

1. Paul is a baseball player _____ position is shortstop.
   위치/자리

2. The cat _____ is jumping on the roof is mine.
   지붕

3. The man _____ you saw the other day is my uncle.
   지난 번

B 밑줄 친 관계대명사절이 꾸며주는 선행사(명사)를 찾아 동그라미 하세요.

1. They use the machine <u>that Jeremy invented</u>.

2. The students <u>who study in my classroom</u> are very kind.

3. I read the book <u>which you lent me</u>.

4. I know the woman <u>whose hair is very long</u>.

5. I need a room <u>which overlooks the sea</u>.
   내려다보다

Unit 14 형용사절

C 선행사를 꾸며주는 관계대명사로써 자연스러운 것을 고르세요.

1 I like the food (whom / that) I ate in the restaurant.

2 He is the scientist (whom / which) I respect.
   존경하다

3 This is the report (which / who) I have to read.

4 The department store (that / whom) I visited was near my house.
   백화점

5 We found the hotel (whom / which) we could stay in.

D 밑줄 친 선행사를 꾸며주는 형용사절을 사용해서 두 문장을 하나로 연결하세요.

> 보기 The man is a lawyer. He lives next door.
> → The man who (that) lives next door is a lawyer.

1 This is the bus. It goes to my hometown.
   → _____

2 The cell phone is Mary's. Its color is white.
   → _____

3 A kiwi is a bird. It lives in New Zealand.
   → _____

4 The boy is Sam. He gets the best grades.
                                성적
   → _____

E 밑줄 친 관계대명사를 올바르게 고쳐 쓰세요.

1 The bag <u>who</u> I bought is not expensive.
   비싼
   → The bag _____ I bought is not expensive.

2 Do you know the woman <u>which</u> Ian introduced to us?
   → Do you know the woman _____ Ian introduced to us?

3 We have a new kitten <u>whom</u> fur is white and black.
   새끼 고양이   털
   → We have a new kitten _____ fur is white and black.

4 It is hard to spend the money <u>whose</u> I earn.
   (돈을)쓰다
   → It is hard to spend the money _____ I earn.
                                                       벌다

5 She knows the man <u>which</u> is sitting next to the window.
   → She knows the man _____ is sitting next to the window.

F 주어진 단어들을 바르게 배열하여 문장을 완성하세요. (참고: 영어는 항상 '주어'를 먼저 찾아야 해요.)

1 Jane used to teach / the subject / History is / that

   → _____

   (역사는 Jane이 가르치던 과목이다.)

2 I trust / Erik and Erica are / whom / the friends

   → _____

   (Erik과 Erica는 내가 믿는 친구들이다.)

3 we bought last year / This is / which / the house

   → _____

   (이곳이 우리가 작년에 산 집이다.)

4 a movie star / whose / brother is / I know the girl

   → _____

   (나는 오빠가 영화배우인 소녀를 안다.)

Unit 14 형용사절

Part 3 Writing Practice

A 주어진 단어들을 활용하여 문장을 영작하세요.

build 짓다	building 건물	eat 먹다	grandfather 할아버지
ice cream 아이스크림	know 알다	look for 찾다	decision 결정
man 남자	math 수학	pretty 예쁜	you made 네가 한(내린)
teacher 선생님	tell 말하다	woman 여자	teach 가르치다

1 우리는 그들이 찾고 있는 그 여자를 모른다. (the woman who(m)~)

→ _____

(우리는 / 모른다 / 그 여자를 / 그들이 / 찾고 있는)

2 네가 한 결정을 내게 말해줄 수 있니? (the decision which~)

→ _____

(할 수 있니 / 너는 / 말하다 / 내게 / 결정을 / 네가 한)

3 자신의 자동차를 도난당한 남자가 있다. (There is~)(man whose car~)

→ _____

(있다 / 남자가 / 자신의 자동차를 / 도난당한)

4 이것이 나의 할아버지가 지은 건물이다. (the building that~)

→ _____

(이것이 / 이다 / 건물 / 나의 할아버지가 / 지은)

5 아이스크림을 먹고 있는 소녀는 Anna 이다. (the girl who~)

→ _____

(소녀는 / 먹고 있는 / 아이스크림을 / Anna 이다)

6 Mr. Jenkins는 수학을 가르치는 선생님이다. (the teacher who~)

→ _____

(Jenkins씨는 / 이다 / 선생님 / 가르치는 / 수학을)

MUST-HAVE 3

B 주어진 단어들을 활용하여 단락을 완성하세요.

a lot of 많은	badminton court 배드민턴 코트	close 가까운	doctor 의사
hospital 병원	near 근처에	park 공원	several 여러 가지의
there 거기서	uncle 삼촌	use 사용하다	work 일하다

1 Yesterday, I had a little fever. _____
　　　　　　　　　　　　　　　열　　　　　(나는 / 갔다 / 병원에 / 가까운 /

_____. _____.
내 집에서)　　　　(그 의사는 / 일하는 / 거기서 / 이다 / 내 삼촌)

So I always go there when I'm sick.

2 _____.
(그 공원은 / 근처에 있는 / 우리 집 / 가지고 있다 / 많은 / 나무들)

In the park, there are _____.
(여러 개의 / 배드민턴 코트가 / 우리가 / 사용할 수 있는)

Many people enjoy taking a walk or playing badminton in the park.
　　　　　　　　　　　　　　　　산책하는 것

C 그림을 묘사해 보세요.

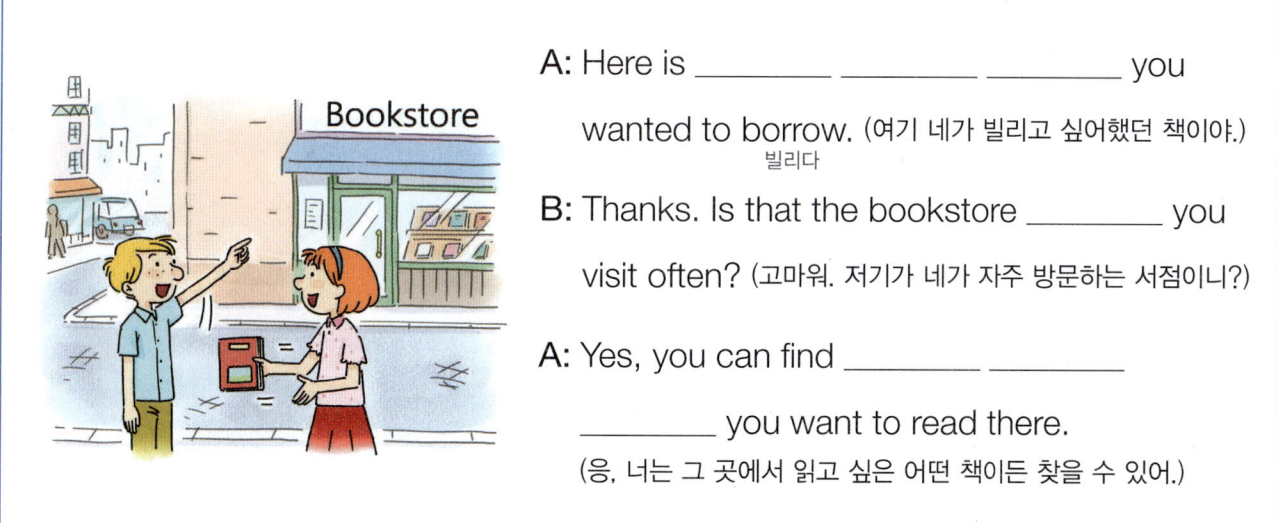

A: Here is _____ _____ _____ you wanted to borrow. (여기 네가 빌리고 싶어했던 책이야.)
　　　　　　　　　　　　　　　　　　　빌리다

B: Thanks. Is that the bookstore _____ you visit often? (고마워. 저기가 네가 자주 방문하는 서점이니?)

A: Yes, you can find _____ _____ _____ you want to read there.
(응, 너는 그 곳에서 읽고 싶은 어떤 책이든 찾을 수 있어.)

* 주요 어휘는 Word Test p.118에서 한 번 더 연습하세요.

Unit 15 복합관계사

Part 1 Grammar Point

A
① 의문사와 '-ever'를 혼합해 만든 말을 복합어(혼합어)라고 합니다.
② 이 복합어는 복합관계대명사와 복합관계부사로 나누어 사용합니다.
③ '-ever'를 붙인 이 복합어들은 '~든지' 또는 '~하더라도'의 의미로 쓰입니다.

복합관계사		의미
복합관계대명사	whatever	무엇이든지 (부정: 정해지지 않음)
		무엇을 ~하더라도 (양보)
	whoever	누구든지 (부정)
		누가 ~하더라도 (양보)
	whichever	~하는 어떤 것이든지 (부정)
		어떤 것을 ~하더라도 (양보)
	whomever	누구를 ~하던지 (부정)
		누구를 ~하더라도 (양보)
복합관계부사	whenever	~할 때마다 (부정)
		언제 ~하더라도 (양보)
	wherever	어디든지 (부정)
		어디서 ~하더라도 (양보)
	however	어떻게 ~하더라도 (however + S + V)
		아무리 ~하더라도 (however + 형용사/부사)

B 복합관계대명사는 **주어, 목적어, 보어**로 사용할 수 있어요.

- **Whoever** comes first will get a prize. 　 누구든 먼저 오는 사람이 상을 받을 것이다. (주어)
- I understand, **whatever** you do. 　 네가 무엇을 하든, 나는 이해한다. (목적어)
- A witch can become **whatever** she wants. 　 마녀는 원하는 무엇으로든 변할 수 있다. (보어)

C 복합관계부사는 내용상 동사를 수식하는 **부사**의 역할을 합니다.

- I play soccer **whenever** I get the chance. 　 나는 기회가 있을 때마다 축구를 한다.
  (= every time)
- Please sit **wherever** you feel comfortable. 　 어디든 편한 곳에 앉으세요.
  (= any place where)

Part 2 Grammar Exercise

A ① 주어진 상황과 가장 적합한 복합관계사를 고르세요.

however	whichever	whoever
아무리 ~해도	어느 쪽을 하든	누구든 ~하는 사람(들)

② 내용이 자연스럽게 되도록 문장을 완성하세요.

1. _____ wants the book, take it!

2. _____ you prefer, I will buy it for you.

3. _____ hungry you may be, you should not eat fast.

B 해석이 가장 자연스러운 복합관계사를 고르세요.

1. (However / Whichever) you take, you won't regret it.
   후회하다

2. (Whomever / Whatever) you do, I will trust you.
   신뢰하다

3. (Whomever / However) you invite, I won't disagree.
   동의하지 않다

4. (Whatever / However) hard you try, it is impossible to stop time.

5. Take a seat (wherever / whatever) you like.

Unit 15 복합관계사

C 밑줄 친 부분의 해석을 살려서 전체 해석을 완성하세요.

1 However cold it is outside, I have to go out.
   → _____, 나는 외출해야 한다.

2 You can do whatever you want.
   → 너는 _____ 할 수 있다.

3 Wherever you want to go, I will go with you.
   → _____, 나는 너와 함께 갈 것이다.

4 Whoever may say so, you need not believe it.
   → _____, 너는 그 말을 믿을 필요는 없다.

5 I will be there whenever you call me.
   → 나는 _____ 거기에 있을 것이다.

D 밑줄 친 복합관계사보다 내용상 더 자연스러운 복합관계사로 고치세요.

> 보기 Whenever you support, I will follow you.
> → Whomever you support, I will follow you.

1 Wherever breaks the law will be punished.
   → _____ breaks the law will be punished.

2 Whatever you stay, I will be with you.
   → _____ you stay, I will be with you.

3 Whichever I invited, she didn't welcome.
   → _____ I invited, she didn't welcome.

4 Wherever you think, it is not her fault.
   → _____ you think, it is not her fault.

E 다음 두 문장이 자연스러운 문장이 되도록 연결하세요.

1. Wherever she drives, • • he can't change her mind.

2. Whichever you choose, • • she has a good sense of direction.
   선택하다   감각   방향

3. Whatever she wants to be, • • you won't regret it.

4. Whoever you meet, • • she will succeed.
                                        성공하다

5. However hard he may try, • • it is important to be polite.
   열심히   예의바른

F 주어진 단어들을 바르게 배열하여 문장을 완성하세요. (참고: 영어는 항상 '주어'를 먼저 찾아야 해요.)

1. you should / you go, / Wherever / have your ID card

   → _____

   (네가 어딜 가든, 너는 신분증이 있어야 한다.)

2. too much / you eat, / Whatever / don't eat

   → _____

   (네가 무엇을 먹든지, 너무 많이 먹지 마라.)

3. you are, / you should / However disappointed / try again

   → _____

   (네가 아무리 실망해도, 너는 다시 한 번 시도해봐야 한다.)

4. she will be / Whichever / the winner / she picks,
                                                    고르다

   → _____

   (그녀는 어떤 것을 고르든지, 승자가 될 것이다.)

Unit 15 복합관계사

Part 3 Writing Practice

A 주어진 단어들을 활용하여 문장을 영작하세요.

anyone 누구, 아무	beautiful 아름다운	buy 사다	check 점검하다
dress 옷을 입다	easy 쉬운	fight 싸우다	fix 고치다
hand 손	look ~처럼 보인다	play with ~와 놀다	question 문제
should ~해야 하다	twice 두 번	wash 씻다	watch 시계

1 그녀는 어떤 옷을 입든, 아름다워 보인다. (Whatever~ 또는 Whichever~)

→ _____

(어떤 것이든지 / 그녀는 / 옷을 입다 / (그녀는) / 보인다 / 아름다운)

2 네가 무엇을 보았든지, 아무에게도 말하면 안 된다. (Whatever~)

→ _____

(무엇이든지 / 네가 / 보았다 / (너는) / 하면 안 된다 / 말하다 / 아무에게도)

3 네가 누구와 놀든지, 싸우면 안 된다. (Whomever~ 또는 Whoever~)

→ _____

(누구든 / 네가 / ~와 놀다 / (너는) / 싸우면 안 된다)

4 그 문제가 아무리 쉬워도, 너는 두 번 점검해야 한다. (However~)

→ _____

(아무리 쉬워도 / 그 문제가 / 이다 / 너는 / 점검해야 한다 / (그것을) / 두 번)

5 집에 올 때마다 손을 씻어라. (Wash로 시작하는 명령문)(whenever~)

→ _____

(씻어라 / 너의 손을 / ~할 때마다 / (네가) / 집에 오다)

6 네가 그 시계를 어디서 샀든지, 나는 그것을 고칠 수 있다. (Wherever~)

→ _____

(어디에서 ~하더라도 / 네가 / 샀다 / 그 시계를 / 나는 / 고칠 수 있다 / 그것을)

MUST-HAVE 3

B 주어진 단어들을 활용하여 단락을 완성하세요.

| at night 밤에 | believe 믿다 | change 바꾸다 | follow 따라오다 | go out 외출하다 |
| hard 열심히 | mind 마음 | say 말하다 | stranger 낯선 사람 | try 노력하다 |

1 Collin is lying to us all the time. _____
   거짓말하는 중   (무엇이든지 / 그가 말하다 / 우리는 /

_____. _____
믿지 않는다 / 그것을)   (아무리 ~하더라도 / 열심히 / 그가 / 노력하다 / (그는) /

_____.
할 수 없다 / 바꾸다 / 우리의 마음을)

2 There are two basic rules for your safety. _____
                              안전   (~할 때마다 /

_____, call the police. _____
낯선 사람이 / 따라오다 / 너를)   (~할 때마다 /

_____, let your family know where you are going.
네가 외출할 때 / 밤에)

C 그림을 묘사해 보세요.

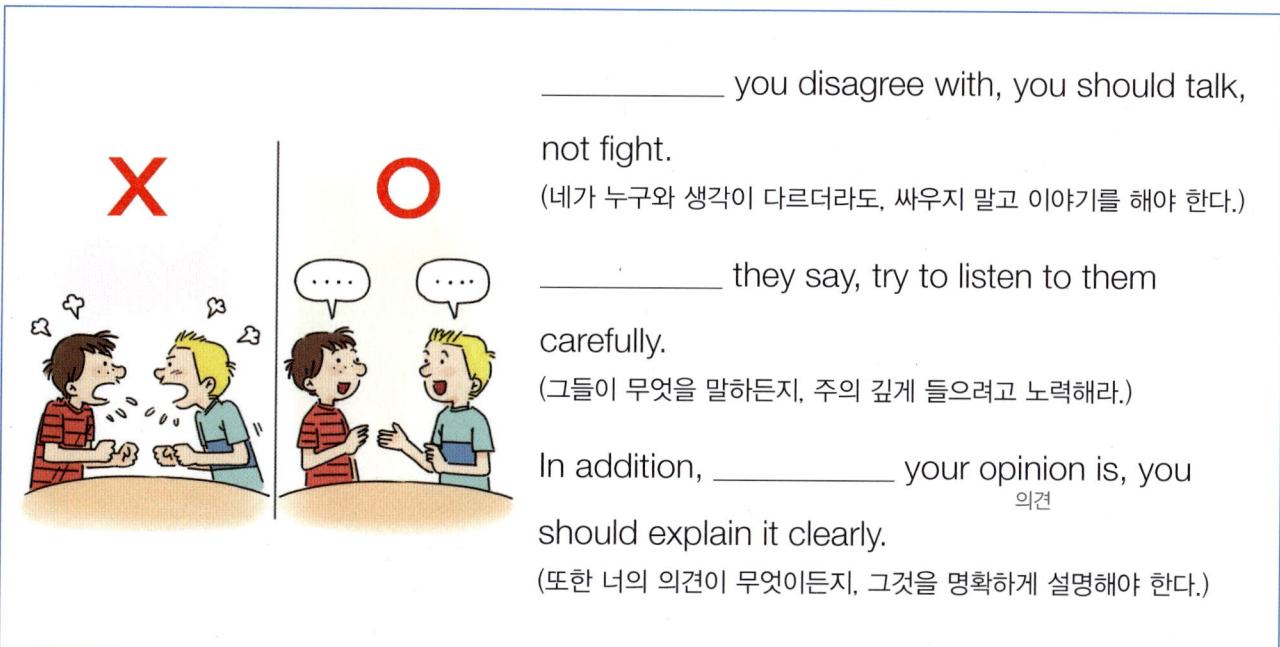

_____ you disagree with, you should talk, not fight.
(네가 누구와 생각이 다르더라도, 싸우지 말고 이야기를 해야 한다.)

_____ they say, try to listen to them carefully.
(그들이 무엇을 말하든지, 주의 깊게 들으려고 노력해라.)

In addition, _____ your opinion is, you
                              의견
should explain it clearly.
(또한 너의 의견이 무엇이든지, 그것을 명확하게 설명해야 한다.)

* 주요 어휘는 Word Test p.119에서 한 번 더 연습하세요.

Review 05 Report

A 아래 표를 참고하여, 혼자하는 여행의 장단점을 제시하는 글에 들어갈 내용을 정리하세요.

Advantages 장점(들)	Disadvantages 단점(들)
very much freedom; go wherever, do whatever (자유)	costs more money (비용이 들다); traveling with others can split the cost (나누다)
new friends; meet new people who they get along with	lonely (외로운); no one who they can have meals with
more time to refresh themselves	dangerous; many cases of robbery (강도)

OUTLINE

Title   Traveling Alone (여행하는 것)

Introduction   has both advantages and disadvantages

Body   **I think that traveling alone,**

- has very much freedom; go _____ and do _____ they want
- make new friends; meet new people _____ they get along with
- can have more time to refresh themselves

However, I think _____ traveling alone,

- costs more money; traveling with others can split the cost
- can be lonely; have no one _____ they can have meals with
- I heard that it could be dangerous; many cases of robbery

Conclusion   should think carefully if they are going to travel alone or not

---

advantage 장점   cost 비용   disadvantage 단점   freedom 자유
lonely 외로운   refresh 생기를 되찾다   robbery 강도

MUST-HAVE 3

B 아웃라인을 바탕으로 혼자하는 여행의 장단점을 제시하는 글을 완성하세요.

Traveling Alone — Title

    Traveling alone has _____. — Introduction

    I _____ traveling alone has very much freedom. Travelers who travel alone can _____. In addition, they can have more chances to make new friends. They can _____. They can have more time to refresh themselves as well.
생기를 되찾게 하다

    However, _____ traveling alone costs more money since traveling with others can split the cost. And it can be lonely. They could have no one _____. Also, I _____ it could be dangerous because there are many cases of robbery.

— Body

    For these reasons, travelers should think carefully _____ _____. — Conclusion

✏️ 아래 내용을 모두 잘 학습하였으면 □안에 ✔하세요.

☐ 명사절을 문장 안에서 주어, 목적어로 맞게 사용하였다.

☐ 형용사절을 맞게 사용하였다.

☐ 복합관계사(wherever, whatever)를 사용하여 그 의미를 맞게 표현하였다.

Appendix

불규칙 변화 동사표

A-A-A형

원형	과거	과거분사	원형	과거	과거분사
bet	bet	bet	let	let	let
cost	cost	cost	put	put	put
cut	cut	cut	read	read	read
fit	fit	fit	set	set	set
hit	hit	hit	shut	shut	shut
hurt	hurt	hurt	spread	spread	spread

A-B-A형

원형	과거	과거분사	원형	과거	과거분사
become	became	become	run	ran	run
come	came	come			

A-B-B형

원형	과거	과거분사	원형	과거	과거분사
bend	bent	bent	have	had	had
bring	brought	brought	hear	heard	heard
build	built	built	hold	held	held
burn	burned/burnt	burned/burnt	keep	kept	kept
buy	bought	bought	lay	laid	laid
catch	caught	caught	lead	led	led
deal	dealt	dealt	leave	left	left
dive	dived/dove	dived	lend	lent	lent
dream	dreamed/dreamt	dreamed/dreamt	light	lighted/lit	lighted/lit
feed	fed	fed	lose	lost	lost
feel	felt	felt	make	made	made
fight	fought	fought	mean	meant	meant
find	found	found	meet	met	met
get	got	gotten/got	pay	paid	paid
hang	hung	hung	say	said	said

sell	sold	sold	stand	stood	stood
send	sent	sent	stick	stuck	stuck
shine	shone	shone	strike	struck	stricken/struck
shoot	shot	shot	swing	swung	swung
sit	sat	sat	teach	taught	taught
sleep	slept	slept	tell	told	told
slide	slid	slid	think	thought	thought
speed	sped/speeded	sped/speeded	understand	understood	understood
spend	spent	spent	win	won	won

A-B-C형

원형	과거	과거분사	원형	과거	과거분사
awake	awoke	awoken	hide	hid	hidden
be	was/were	been	know	knew	known
begin	began	begun	lie	lay	lain
bite	bit	bitten	ride	rode	ridden
blow	blew	blown	ring	rang	rung
break	broke	broken	rise	rose	risen
choose	chose	chosen	see	saw	seen
do	did	done	shake	shook	shaken
draw	drew	drawn	show	showed	shown
drink	drank	drunk	sing	sang	sung
drive	drove	driven	sink	sank	sunk
eat	ate	eaten	speak	spoke	spoken
fall	fell	fallen	spring	sprang	sprung
fly	flew	flown	steal	stole	stolen
forget	forgot	forgotten	swim	swam	swum
forgive	forgave	forgiven	take	took	taken
freeze	froze	frozen	throw	threw	thrown
give	gave	given	wake	woke	woken
go	went	gone	wear	wore	worn
grow	grew	grown	write	wrote	written

Appendix

부사접속사의 종류

접속사	뜻	접속사	뜻
after	~후에	whereas	~에 반하여
before	~전에	unless	~하지 않으면
when	~할 때	if	만일 ~면
while	~하는 동안에	only if	오직 ~면
as	~할 때 (동시에 일어나는 상황)	as if	마치 ~처럼
by the time	~무렵에는, 그때까지	whether or not	~인지 아닌지
since	~이래로, ~이 이유로	even if	비록 ~일지라도
until	~때까지	provided (that)	다만 ~한다면
as soon as	~하자마자 곧	in case (that)	만일의 경우를 대비해서
once	일단, 일찍이, 한번	supposing	만일 ~이라면
as long as	~하는 한	than	~보다
whenever	~할 때는 언제든지	whenever	언제나
every time	~할 때마다	wherever	어디든지
(the) first time (that)	처음 ~할 때/~일 때	whichever	어느 것이든, 어느 쪽이든
because	~ 때문에	whoever	누가 ~하더라도
now that	이제 ~해서, 이제 ~한 이상	so~that	너무 ~해서 ~하다
even though	비록 ~이지만	such~that	너무 ~해서 ~하다
although	비록 ~이지만		
though	비록 ~이지만		

Word Test
Book 3

MUST-HAVE Grammar

Word Test

■ 다음 단어를 영어는 한글로, 한글은 영어로 바꿔 쓰세요.

Unit 01   정답 pp. 12-13

1. at least _____
2. cheat _____
3. lift _____
4. memorize _____
5. miss _____
6. 시험에서 _____
7. 액션 _____
8. 영화 _____
9. 친절 _____
10. 태워다 주다 _____

Unit 02   정답 pp. 18-19

1. move _____
2. pet shop _____
3. pink _____
4. plant pot _____
5. vet _____
6. 가져가다 _____
7. 사진을 찍다 _____
8. 여행을 가다 _____
9. 우산 _____
10. (잠시) 들르다 _____

112

MUST-HAVE 3

■ 다음 단어를 영어는 한글로, 한글은 영어로 바꿔 쓰세요.

Unit 03 정답 pp. 24-25

1. at first _____
2. coach _____
3. for a minute _____
4. take a class _____
5. walk _____
6. 가게 _____
7. 내일 _____
8. 사전 _____
9. 주말 _____
10. (전화를) 받다 _____

Unit 04 정답 pp. 32-33

1. area _____
2. catch _____
3. everything _____
4. keep regular hours _____
5. skateboard _____
6. 낮잠을 자다 _____
7. 때문에 _____
8. 마음 _____
9. 약속을 어기다 _____
10. 최선을 다하다 _____

■ 다음 단어를 영어는 한글로, 한글은 영어로 바꿔 쓰세요.

Unit 05 정답 pp. 38-39

1 every time _____

2 lake _____

3 own _____

4 sometimes _____

5 swimmer _____

6 등산하러 가다 _____

7 연습하다 _____

8 오래 전에는 _____

9 유명한 _____

10 점심 _____

Unit 06 정답 pp. 44-45

1 all right _____

2 leading role _____

3 perform _____

4 ready _____

5 take a shower _____

6 말하다 _____

7 아래층으로 _____

8 열심히 하다 _____

9 잠자리에 들다 _____

10 (잠을) 깨다 _____

MUST-HAVE 3

■ 다음 단어를 영어는 한글로, 한글은 영어로 바꿔 쓰세요.

Unit 07 정답 pp. 52-53

1 become clear _____

2 drawing _____

3 feel better _____

4 get injured _____

5 keep quiet _____

6 계속하다 _____

7 날씨 _____

8 눈이 내리다 _____

9 약을 먹다 _____

10 여행 _____

Unit 08 정답 pp. 58-59

1 album _____

2 dessert _____

3 hand _____

4 lend _____

5 useful _____

6 보여주다 _____

7 사진 _____

8 정보 _____

9 지금은 _____

10 책가방 _____

115

■ 다음 단어를 영어는 한글로, 한글은 영어로 바꿔 쓰세요.

Unit 09   정답 pp. 64-65

1 bully   _____

2 finish   _____

3 living room   _____

4 sister   _____

5 talk about   _____

6 도망가다   _____

7 사람들   _____

8 아침 식사   _____

9 울다   _____

10 최종의   _____

Unit 10   정답 pp. 72-73

1 all   _____

2 just   _____

3 outdoor activity _____

4 perfect score   _____

5 since   _____

6 고향   _____

7 수학   _____

8 유치원   _____

9 태어나다   _____

10 햇빛   _____

■ 다음 단어를 영어는 한글로, 한글은 영어로 바꿔 쓰세요.

Unit 11 정답 pp.78-79

1 bright _____

2 busy _____

3 comic book _____

4 know _____

5 moon _____

6 가수 _____

7 긴 _____

8 남자 형제 _____

9 드레스 _____

10 아름다운 _____

Unit 12 정답 pp.84-85

1 fly around _____

2 in the river _____

3 make a friend _____

4 new _____

5 write _____

6 녹색의 _____

7 모기 _____

8 미래에 _____

9 우주에 _____

10 잎 _____

■ 다음 단어를 영어는 한글로, 한글은 영어로 바꿔 쓰세요.

Unit 13   정답 pp. 92-93

1. great _____
2. innocent _____
3. point _____
4. true _____
5. wallet _____
6. 반장 _____
7. 버스를 타다 _____
8. 중고의 _____
9. 지난번에 _____
10. 피아니스트 _____

Unit 14   정답 pp. 98-99

1. build _____
2. close _____
3. make a decision _____
4. pretty _____
5. work _____
6. 남자 _____
7. 삼촌 _____
8. 여러 가지의 _____
9. 찾다 _____
10. 할아버지 _____

■ 다음 단어를 영어는 한글로, 한글은 영어로 바꿔 쓰세요.

Unit 15 정답 pp.104-105

1 hard _____

2 play with _____

3 should _____

4 stranger _____

5 twice _____

6 노력하다 _____

7 누구, 아무 _____

8 바꾸다 _____

9 외출하다 _____

10 문제 _____

Answer Key
Book 3

MUST-HAVE Grammar

Answer Key

Unit 01
Grammar Exercise pp. 09-11

A
1. May / use
2. will / go
3. Can / lift

B
1. attend
2. be
3. solve
4. take
5. break

C
1. Can she jump rope very well?
2. Alex will not walk his dog today. OR
   Alex won't walk his dog today.
3. You may not use my computer.
4. Must all visitors follow the rules? OR
   Do all visitors have to follow the rules?
5. They may not touch this statue.

D
1. 그들은 이번 주에 교실을 청소할 것이다.
2. 나는 그 속담을 이해할 수 있다.
3. 너는 이번 주 주말까지 에세이를 써도 된다.
4. Rachel은 내일까지 이 책을 반납할 것이다.
5. 그 유령이야기는 사실일지도 모른다.

E
1. must
2. may not
3. will not
4. must not
5. can

F
1. I can't open this door.
2. She may allow us to go to a movie.
3. You must not wear shoes inside the room.
4. I won't make this mistake again.

Writing Practice pp. 12-13

A
1. You may(can) have one more cookie.
2. You must memorize at least ten words a day.
3. Can you lift this box with one hand?
4. I will not forget your kindness. OR
   I won't forget your kindness.
5. The cat can not climb a tree. OR
   The cat cannot(can't) climb a tree.
6. You must not cheat on the exam.

B
1. You must see this action movie /
   you will enjoy their actions OR
   you'll enjoy their actions
2. We may miss the school bus /
   my mom will drive us to school

C
may / invite
must / finish
will

Unit 02
Grammar Exercise pp. 15-17

A
1. won't
2. going to
3. Will / move

B

1. going
2. be
3. skip
4. buy
5. to stay

C

1. am going to help
2. is not going to open
3. are not going to lie
4. are going to eat

D

1. Q: Will Sandra give you a hand?
   A: No, she will not. OR
   No, she won't
2. Q: Is Jim going to see the dentist?
   A: Yes, he is.
3. Q: Will it be cloudy and windy?
   A: Yes, it will.
4. Q: Are they going to arrive at 9 p.m.?
   A: No, they are not. OR
   No, they aren't.

E

1. The bus is going to leave in ten minutes.
2. It will snow next week.
3. Are you going to take the subway tomorrow?
4. I will not go swimming this weekend. OR
   I won't go swimming this weekend.

F

1. I will call you next week.
2. He is going to stay in Seoul for two weeks.
3. The doctor is going to see you in a minute.
4. Will you give me one more chance?

Writing Practice pp. 18-19

A

1. Ken is going to play tennis this morning.
2. Bob is going to take pictures at the party.
3. I will not take this pink umbrella. OR
   I won't take this pink umbrella.
4. Is she going to wear a blue dress tomorrow?
5. Are you going to move the plant pot here?
6. He will go on a trip with his family.

B

1. We are going to study together on the weekend /
   The school library will not open this weekend OR
   The school library won't open this weekend
2. I am going to take him to the vet /
   we will stop by a pet shop to buy some food

C

am / going / to

will / be

will / will

Unit 03

Grammar Exercise pp. 21-23

A

1. Can / climb up
2. be able to / save
3. May / come in

B

1. might
2. Can
3. could
4. able to
5. may

C

1. won't be able to

Answer Key

2. may be able to
3. will not be able to
4. will be able to

D

1. There could be some mistakes in his homework.
2. We will be able to enjoy the picnic next week.
3. That may be another chance for you.
4. They were able to find the way to the station.

E

1. Is Gary able to write a good essay?
2. It may not be sunny tomorrow morning.
3. I was not able to take the ski class. OR
   I wasn't able to take the ski class.
4. Was she able to finish her test?
5. They could not arrive here on time. OR
   They couldn't arrive here on time.

F

1. May I try on the yellow shirt?
2. She might know how to play chess.
3. Were you able to get enough sleep last night?
4. You can start the game after dinner.

Writing Practice pp. 24-25

A

1. May I use your dictionary for a minute?
2. We might lose the match.
3. I could not walk without his help. OR
   I couldn't walk without his help.
4. David will be able to come here tomorrow.
5. You may be able to take a class next year.
6. I could not answer your call. OR
   I couldn't answer your call.

B

1. The store may not open this weekend /
   We can do online shopping
2. It may not be easy at first /
   I can do it with a good coach's help

C

can't(cannot) / live

may

won't / be / able / to

can / cause

Review 01 pp. 26-27

A

will

going / to

can

do

be

B

some plans for my summer vacation

am going to take swimming lessons

will take part in

am going to read as many books as possible

can learn many things

will do volunteer work

might be hard

will be helpful

will

Unit 04
Grammar Exercise pp. 29-31

A

1. have to / fix
2. should / apologize
3. must not / park

B
1. has to
2. have to
3. have to
4. have to
5. has to

C
1. don't have to
2. must not
3. doesn't have to
4. should

D
1. He had to cancel his appointment with the doctor.
2. They will have to stop by the gas station soon.
3. Andy has to finish his speech within five minutes.
4. She had to help her brother care for his son.

E
1. She did not have to eat a late-night snack. OR
   She didn't have to eat a late-night snack.
2. Should they stop smoking?
3. Must Randy do the dishes for Mom? OR
   Does Randy have to do the dishes for Mom?
4. He does not have to fly to New York tomorrow. OR
   He doesn't have to fly to New York tomorrow.

F
1. You don't have to worry about your future.
2. We should not tell anyone about the secret.
3. People must not use bad words to children.
4. Should I bring my student ID tomorrow?

Writing Practice pp. 32-33

A
1. You should not break your promise.
2. You will have to wait for ten minutes.
3. We don't have to change our mind.
4. They must not ride their skateboards in this area.
5. She had to skip breakfast to catch the bus.
6. You should do your best in everything.

B
1. You should go home and take a nap /
   I must keep regular hours
2. He had to move here because of his school /
   he doesn't have to take a long walk to school

C
have / to / leave
must / arrive
don't / have / to / hurry

Unit 05
Grammar Exercise pp. 35-37

A
1. used to / be
2. would / take care of
3. would rather / take

B
1. used to
2. used to
3. would
4. used to
5. would rather

C
1. would like to
2. would rather
3. would
4. used to

Answer Key

D
1. Gary used to be a film director.
2. I would rather stay poor than steal things. OR
   I'd rather stay poor than steal things.
3. I would like to make an appointment with Dr. Smith. OR
   I'd like to make an appointment with Dr. Smith.
4. The restaurant would serve traditional food.

E
1. I would like to be a famous actor. OR
   I'd like to be a famous actor.
2. She would rather stay home alone. OR
   She'd rather stay home alone.
3. I would like to buy those small toys. OR
   I'd like to buy those small toys.
4. We would rather play hide-and-seek on the playground. OR
   We'd rather play hide-and-seek on the playground.

F
1. He would drink a lot of water after a game.
2. Jane used to be shy when she was young.
3. We would rather eat out than order in.
4. Would you like to live in the country?

Writing Practice pp. 38-39

A
1. He used to have his own car.
2. They would sometimes go hiking.
3. The lake used to be clean a long time ago.
4. I would rather stay (at) home. OR
   I'd rather stay (at) home.
5. I would like to drink orange juice. OR
   I'd like to drink orange juice.
6. He used to take a walk after lunch every time.

B
1. I used to be a famous swimmer /
   I used to practice a lot in the water every day
2. Jack would play computer games more than 2(two) hours /
   He would rather play soccer than play computer games OR
   He'd rather play soccer than play computer games

C
used / to / be
would / climb
would / read

Unit 06
Grammar Exercise pp. 41-43

A
1. when
2. After
3. until

B
1. until
2. because
3. Before
4. after
5. When

C
1. when she was five.
2. until I come back.
3. when I left home.
4. after I graduate.
5. because the road was too muddy.

D
1. before

2. until
3. When
4. because
5. after

E
1. began
2. ended
3. get
4. stops

F
1. When spring came, flowers began to bloom.
2. After Fred moved to a city, I never saw him.
3. Jane moved there because her sister lived near there.
4. I didn't go to sleep until my dad came home.

Writing Practice pp. 44-45

A
1. Mike helped his mom because she was busy.
2. I will be with you until everything is all right. OR I'll be with you until everything is all right.
3. When I woke up, I found something wrong.
4. Betty thinks too much before she says something.
5. You may(can) watch TV until dinner is ready.
6. I came downstairs after I took a shower.

B
1. He came home after I went to sleep /
   When I woke up this morning, he was not home
   OR
   When I woke up this morning, he wasn't home
2. He tried hard because he wanted to perform in the play /
   He was happy when he won the leading role

C
When / didn't
decided / after
exercise / because

Review 02 pp. 46-47

A
should
used / to
must / before
would
would

B
should make some promises to myself
should get up at 7
used to get up at 8
middle school begins at 8
must do my homework before I do other things
would play computer games
would sometimes forget to do my homework

Unit 07
Grammar Exercise pp. 49-51

A
1. As long as
2. As soon as
3. Even though

B
1. As soon as
2. Even though
3. as long as
4. Even though
5. as soon as

Answer Key

C

1. as long as you need it.
2. as soon as I saw the boy.
3. even if he is tired.
4. even though it was new.
5. as long as it doesn't rain.

D

1. as soon as
2. as long as
3. even though
4. as long as
5. even though

E

1. wash
2. was
3. works
4. are

F

1. As long as you are okay, I am fine, too.
2. Even though Jake is thin, he is pretty strong.
3. As soon as we arrived home, it began to rain.
4. As long as the bus is not late, I will arrive at school on time.

Writing Practice pp. 52-53

A

1. Even though the weather was cold, she went swimming.
2. As long as you have a friend, you are happy.
3. As soon as he took some medicine, he felt better.
4. I will keep volunteering as long as I have time.
5. The drawing was very expensive even though it was not wonderful. OR
   The drawing was very expensive even though it wasn't wonderful.
6. You can stay here as long as you keep quiet.

B

1. He will play even though he got injured /
   As long as he can play, he will do his best
2. As soon as it stops snowing, they will continue their journey /
   as soon as the weather becomes clear

C

Even / though
As / long / as

Unit 08
Grammar Exercise pp. 55-57

A

1. gave
2. sent
3. bought

B

1. me many books
2. us some books
3. you beautiful scenery
4. me his notebook
5. him a sweater

C

1. ② ① ③
2. ① ③ ②
2. ③ ② ④ ①
3. ① ② ④ ③

D

1. Donna gave her old skirts to them.
2. My mother cooked some delicious spaghetti for us.

3. I will lend it to him.

4. Dan bought a brand-new cell phone for his son.

E

1. to
2. for
3. x
4. to
5. for

F

1. They sent me an interesting book.
2. We should show them our passports.
3. Ms. Taylor teaches French to us.
4. My uncle bought a new watch for me.

Writing Practice p. 58-59

A

1. I showed Mac my album.
2. Will you give me a hand?
3. My uncle bought me a backpack.
4. Amy sent us some very useful information.
5. Tina brought us some dessert.
6. I can lend you 10 dollars for now.

B

1. Tony often lends me some good books /
   He gave me the book as a gift
2. Ken sent me some photos /
   he lent me his camera

C

bought / me

sent / to

sent / me

Unit 09

Grammar Exercise pp. 61-63

A

1. see
2. hear
3. Let

B

1. run
2. snore
3. go out / play
4. talk
5. write

C

1. (②) (①) (③)
2. (①) (③) (②)
3. (③) (①) (②)
4. (②) (①) (③)

D

1. let me see
2. helped her son keep OR
   helped her son to keep
3. had the waiter bring
4. let me stay out

E

1. She made me buy some milk for her.
2. They heard him talk on the phone. OR
   They heard him talking on the phone.
3. He let us play the board game after school.
4. We watched her sleep on the couch. OR
   We watched her sleeping on the couch.

F

1. The speech made me fall asleep.
2. I saw a star fall down from the sky.

Answer Key

3. I helped Young prepare for the interview.
4. Ken will let you know what happened.

Writing Practice pp. 64-65

A

1. Our coach had us practice for the final match.
2. Will you help me finish the report? OR
   Will you help me to finish the report?
3. Don't let them bully you.
4. My mother never let me skip breakfast.
5. Cindy heard them talk about her friend. OR
   Cindy heard them talking about her friend.
6. Tammy saw us run away from a big cat. OR
   Tammy saw us running away from a big cat.

B

1. We saw many people take a walk OR
   We saw many people taking a walk /
   We heard many people talk about the weather OR
   We heard many people talking about the weather
2. The movie made me cry /
   I heard my sister cry in the living room OR
   I heard my sister crying in the living room

C

saw / fall OR falling
helped / her / get
helped / her / walk

Review 03 pp. 66-67

A

as / soon / as
gave / me / the / piano
saw / me / play
made / them / smile

B

when I got a surprise present
As soon as
saw a new piano
gave me the piano
was very excited
Even though I was not good at playing the piano
saw me play the piano
made them smile

Unit 10

Grammar Exercise pp. 69-71

A

1. have played
2. has driven
3. has lost

B

1. has / lost
2. have / stayed
3. has / been
4. has / rained
5. have / worked

C

1. Paula has not eaten lunch at that restaurant. OR
   Paula hasn't eaten lunch at that restaurant.
2. Has Brian bought a brand-new suit?
3. Linda has not seen her brother for two months.
   OR
   Linda hasn't seen her brother for two months.
4. Has she talked about the concert with him?
5. Ted has not locked his keys in his car. OR
   Ted hasn't locked his keys in his car.

D

1. snowed

2. have taken
3. went
4. have known

E
1. have had
2. has been
3. have known
4. lived

F
1. I have taken tennis lessons for two years.
2. Have you ever been to another country?
3. We have checked our plan three times.
4. They have never heard such an interesting story.

Writing Practice pp. 72-73

A
1. We have had this old TV since 2002. OR
   We've had this old TV since 2002.
2. Nick has lost his car key.
3. I have just got(gotten) an email from my German friend. OR
   I've just got(gotten) an email from my German friend.
4. They have been friends since preschool. OR
   They've been friends since preschool.
5. I have studied math for three years. OR
   I've studied math for three years.
6. Have you got(gotten) a perfect score on a test? OR
   Have you ever got(gotten) a perfect score on a test?

B
1. Sam has never left his hometown /
   He has lived in his hometown since he was born

2. We have done a lot of outdoor activities OR
   We've done a lot of outdoor activities /
   We have enjoyed all the sunshine OR
   We've enjoyed all the sunshine

C
Have / you / visited
haven't
has / displayed
have / wanted

Unit 11
Grammar Exercise pp. 75-77

A
1. thinner
2. stronger
3. healthier
4. more handsome
5. more famous
6. more
7. later OR latter
8. more interesting

B
faster / bigger / more difficult
1. bigger
2. faster
3. more difficult

C
1. big
2. worse
3. heavier
4. taller and taller

D
1. My desk is longer than yours.
2. I am taller than my younger sister.

Answer Key

3. This year, the temperature is hotter than last year.
4. A laptop is more expensive than a cell phone.

E

1. This city is smaller than that city.
2. That camera is cheaper than this camera.
3. Alex swims faster than Jim.
4. Science is more difficult than math.

F

1. My father is older than my mother.
2. Chinese is not as easy as English.
3. Science is getting more advanced.
4. My computer works more slowly than my friend's.

Writing Practice pp. 78-79

A

1. The sun is brighter than the moon.
2. She knows more about history than me.
3. Kevin is as creative as his brother.
4. The day is getting longer. OR
   The day is getting longer and longer.
5. The red dress is fancier than the yellow dress.
6. The street was getting busier. OR
   The street was getting busier and busier.

B

1. Her voice is more beautiful than /
   My sister likes her as much as I do OR
   My sister likes her as much as I like her
2. Comic books are more interesting than novels /
   The more I read, the more I enjoy.

C

was / better / than

getting / smarter / and / smarter

gets / better / grades

Unit 12
Grammar Exercise pp. 81-83

A

1. many
2. a little
3. a few

B

1. a lot of
2. several
3. a little
4. a number of
5. much

C

1. much
2. many
3. a few
4. much
5. a little

D

1. a couple of cards
2. a little sugar
3. some eggs
4. a lot of pictures

E

1. X
2. much OR plenty of OR a lot of OR lots of
3. a little
4. X
5. many OR a lot of OR a number of OR plenty of

F

1. There were a number of students in the library.
2. Plants need a lot of sunshine to grow.
3. My father took a few days off to go on a trip.

4. Most of the buildings were destroyed in the earthquake.

Writing Practice pp. 84-85

A

1. Ben wrote her a couple of letters.
2. There are a large number of stars in the universe. OR

   There're a large number of stars in the universe.
3. My father does not drink much wine. OR

   My father doesn't drink much wine.
4. There are not many fish in the river. OR

   There aren't many fish in the river.
5. I would like to make a lot of friends in the future. OR

   I'd like to make a lot of friends in the future.
6. I saw a few mosquitoes fly around me. OR

   I saw a few mosquitoes flying around me.

B

1. I have some(a few) problems /

   I do not have much(lots of OR plenty of OR a lot of) money now OR

   I don't have much(lots of OR plenty of OR a lot of) money now
2. several trees in the yard/

   the trees have many(lots of OR plenty of OR a lot of) green leaves

C

many / friends

a / couple / of / teachers

a / lot / of

Review 04 pp. 86-87

A

a / lot / of

ridden

more / efficient

have

B

what I have done

have used a cup

waste a lot of water

have ridden my bike

a more efficient way

I have unplugged the electronics

Unit 13
Grammar Exercise pp. 89-91

A

1. know / that
2. thinks / that
3. heard / that

B

1. 목적어
2. 주어
3. 보어
4. 주어
5. 목적어

C

1. 그녀가 프랑스에서 왔다는 것은
2. 우리가 제2언어를 숙달하는 것은
3. 우리가 두 번째 기회가 있다는 것은 OR

   우리에게 또 다른 기회가 있다는 것은
4. 우리가 규칙을 어기지 말아야 합니다는 것은

D

1. It is necessary that I meet my teacher.
2. It is true that Ralph is married.
3. It is unbelievable that we used to call him a genius.

Answer Key

4. It is common knowledge that the Earth is round.

E
1. She knows that I like her.
2. I thought that I made a mistake.
3. I don't believe that he passed the driving test.
4. I heard that our team won the game.

F
1. Did you hear that Greg became a doctor?
2. I believe that music has a healing effect.
3. I think that you made a big mistake.
4. I remember that she used to be an artist.

Writing Practice pp. 92-93

A
1. We heard that Jessie bought a used car.
2. The important point is that you did your best.
3. He remembers that we helped him the other day.
4. It is not true that Sandy is the class president. OR
   It isn't true that Sandy is the class president. OR
   It's not true that Sandy is the class president.
5. I heard that Frank took the wrong bus.
6. It will not change that you are my friend. OR
   It won't change that you are my friend.

B
1. It was true that he plays the piano very well /
   I think that he will be a great pianist
2. It is not true that he stole my wallet OR
   It isn't true that he stole my wallet OR
   It's not true that he stole my wallet /
   I know that Tom is innocent

C
know / that
I / thought / that
I / believed / that

I / realized / that

Unit 14
Grammar Exercise pp. 95-97

A
1. whose
2. which
3. who(m)

B
1. (the machine)
2. (The students)
3. (the book)
4. (the woman)
5. (a room)

C
1. that
2. whom
3. which
4. that
5. which

D
1. This is the bus which(that) goes to my hometown.
2. The cell phone whose color is white is Mary's. OR
   The cell phone of which the color is white is Mary's.
3. A kiwi is a bird which(that) lives in New Zealand.
4. The boy who(that) gets the best grades is Sam.

E
1. which OR that
2. whom OR who OR that
3. whose OR of which
4. which OR that
5. who OR that

F

1. History is the subject that Jane used to teach.
2. Erik and Erica are the friends whom I trust.
3. This is the house which we bought last year.
4. I know the girl whose brother is a movie star.

Writing Practice pp. 98-99

A

1. We don't know the woman whom(who OR that) they are looking for.
2. Can you tell me the decision which you made?
3. There is the man whose car was stolen.
4. This is the building that my grandfather built.
5. The girl who(that) is eating ice cream is Anna.
6. Mr. Jenkins is the teacher who(that) teaches math.

B

1. I went to the hospital which(that) is close to my house /
   The doctor who(that) works there is my uncle
2. The park which(that) is near my house has a lot of trees /
   there are several badminton courts which(that) we can use OR
   there're several badminton courts which(that) we can use

C

the / book / that(which)
that(which)
any / books / that(which)

Unit 15
Grammar Exercise pp. 101-103

A

1. Whoever
2. Whichever
3. However

B

1. Whichever
2. Whatever
3. Whomever
4. However
5. wherever

C

1. 밖이 아무리 추워도
2. 네가 원하는 것은 무엇이든
3. 네가 어디를 가고 싶든지
4. 누가 그렇게 말하더라도
5. 네가 전화하면 언제든지 (네가 전화할 때마다)

D

1. Whoever
2. Wherever
3. Whoever OR Whomever
4. Whatever

E

1. she has a good sense of direction.
2. you won't regret it.
3. she will succeed.
4. it is important to be polite.
5. he can't change her mind.

F

1. Wherever you go, you should have your ID card.
2. Whatever you eat, don't eat too much.
3. However disappointed you are, you should try

Answer Key

again.
4. Whichever she picks, she will be the winner.

Writing Practice pp. 104-105

A

1. Whatever(Whichever) she dresses, she looks beautiful.
2. Whatever you saw, you should not tell anyone.
3. Whomever(Whoever) you play with, you should not fight.
4. However easy the question is, you should check it twice.
5. Wash your hands whenever you come home.
6. Wherever you bought the watch, I can fix it.

B

1. Whatever he says, we don't believe it /
   However hard he may try, he can't(cannot) change our minds
2. Whenever a stranger follows you /
   Whenever you go out at night

C

Whomever(Whoever)
Whatever
whatever

Review 05 pp. 106-107

A

wherever
whatever
who
that
who

B

both advantages and disadvantages
think that
go wherever and do whatever they want
meet new people who they get along with
I think that
who they can have meals with
heard that
if they are going to travel alone or not